Phil Maggitti

Birman Cats

Everything about Acquisition, Care, Nutrition,
Breeding, Health Care, and Behavior

With 35 Color Photographs

Illustrations by Michele Earle-Bridges

© Copyright 1996 by Barron's Educational
Series, Inc.

All inquiries should be addressed to:
Barron's Educational Series, Inc.
250 Wireless Boulevard
Hauppauge, NY 11788

International Standard Book No. 0-8120-9584-7

Library of Congress Catalog Card No. 96-3265

**Library of Congress Cataloging-in-Publication
Data**
Maggitti, Phil.
    Birman cats : everything about acquisiton,
    care, nutrition, behavior, health care, and
    breeding / Phil Maggitti ; illustrations by Michele
    Earle-Bridges.
        p.   cm.—(A complete pet owner's manual)
    Includes bibliographical references (p.   )
    and index.
    ISBN 0–8120–9584–7
    1. Birman cat. I. Title. II. Series.
SF449.B5M34   1996
636.8′3—dc20   96-3265
                                                    CIP

Printed in Hong Kong

987654321

About the Author:
    Phil Maggitti is a freelance writer and editor living happily ever after in southeastern Pennsylvania with his wife Mary Ann, eight cats, and six pug dogs. He has received a number of awards for his writing, including two awards from the American Horse Council—for best feature article in 1985 and for best personal column in 1986—and one award from the Dog Writers Association of America for best single-breed booklet in 1994.

Other Barron's titles by Phil Maggitti:
Before You Buy That Kitten (1995)
Pugs: A Complete Pet Owner's Manual (1994)
Guide to a Well-behaved Cat (1993)
*Scottish Fold Cats: A Complete Pet Owner's
    Manual* (1993)

Photo Credits
    All of the photographs appearing in this book were taken by Bob Schwartz except for the following: The photograph on page 4 was taken by Richard Katris of Chanan Photography.

Important Note
    When you handle cats, you may sometimes get scratched or bitten. If this happens, have a doctor treat the injuries immediately.
    Make sure your cat receives all the necessary shots and dewormings, otherwise serious danger to the animal and to human health may arise. A few diseases and parasites can be communicated to humans. If your cat shows any signs of illness, you should definitely consult a veterinarian. If you are worried about your own health, see your doctor and tell him or her that you have cats.
    Some people have allergic reactions to cats. If you think you might be allergic, see your doctor before you get a cat.
    It is possible for a cat to cause damage to someone else's property and even to cause accidents. For your own protection you should make sure your insurance covers such eventualities, and you should definitely have liability insurance.

Contents

One kitten's beeper went off right after the photographer said "cheese."

Preface

For a number of years now conventional wisdom has been braying that cats are the most popular pets in the United States. Writer after writer has earnestly declared that at some point during the 1980s, cats replaced dogs as this country's pets of choice. This information has no doubt energized more than a few cat lovers, particularly the nouveau sort, and perhaps it has even chagrined a dog lover or two. Whatever the case, the statement simply is not true, and evidence to the contrary has been available for some time.

A 1987 survey commissioned by the American Veterinary Medical Association (AVMA) revealed that 38.2 percent of all American households owned dogs, while 30.5 percent owned cats. To be sure, cats outnumbered dogs as household pets because people who owned cats tended to own more of them—2.04 per household compared to 1.51 for dogs—but more households preferred the company of dogs

Another survey, this one conducted by the Association of Pet Product Manufacturers of America (APPMA) in 1994, produced virtually the same estimates—36 percent for dogs, 30 percent for cats. The APPMA survey also revealed that the cat population in this country had fallen 5 percent between 1992 and 1994. Indeed, said the APPMA, the number of cat-owning households "has been in a steady decline" since 1990.

This having been said, it can also be said that cats are a supremely snug and unobtrusive fit for the two-career, deferred-child-raising, one-person-households of the 1990s. Unlike dogs, whose needs expand to fill all the available space in your life—the way high-powered software wants to command all the available memory in your computer—cats remain user-friendly on a modest amount of program space. Cats do not have to be taken outside at 5:00 A.M. in a nor'easter, and their owners do not have to turn down a sudden invitation to go sailing off the Florida Keys because it is not safe to leave the cat alone in the chateau overnight. What is more, cats occasion lower medical fees than dogs—by an average of $28.42 per office visit—says the AVMA's most recent survey. Small wonder, then, that these small wonders in fur appear on so many T-shirts, coffee mugs, Christmas cards, book covers, automobile windows, and sofas in late-twentieth-century America. And small wonder that cats are the one pet to have if you are having more than one.

Finally, even if the revelation that cats are this country's most popular pets were true, it would constitute nothing more than a big "so what?" The died-in-the-fur cat lover has traditionally been a nontrendy soul anyway. And, if the truth were known, the best cat lovers have always enjoyed being the underdogs.

For its part the subject of this book, the Birman cat, adds roughly 1,000 new registrations to the rolls of the Cat Fanciers' Association (CFA) each year. Those kittens accounted for 1 percent of CFA's new registrations in 1994. This number established the Birman as the ninth most popular of the 37 breeds that CFA registered.

Phil Maggitti
Fall 1996

The Birman's Sacred History

The Birman, which is also known as the Sacred Cat of Burma, is endowed with the sort of legend guaranteed to amplify its appeal. According to that legend, the Birman was revered in its native land, where people believed that the souls of departed priests returned to their country's temples in the form of these unique cats. One of the temples where the sacred cats dwelled was Lao-Tsun, located on the side of Mount Lugh in western Burma between China and India. In the temple of Lao-Tsun, a priest named Mun-Ha knelt in nightly adoration before a statue of Tsun-Kyan-Kse, the blue-eyed goddess who presided over the transmutation of souls. Each night, as Mun-Ha prayed, a sacred cat named Sinh was at his side.

Legends and Legacies

One evening, the temple of Lao-Tsun was overrun by Siamese invaders who took their fill of booty and took the life of Mun-Ha. Sinh immediately stood guard over his fallen master, with his front paws on Mun-Ha's head, facing the statue of Tsun-Kyan-Kse. As Sinh kept his vigil, a wondrous transformation occurred. His coat, which had been entirely white until that time, took on the golden glow radiating from the statue of Tsun-Kyan-Kse. Then Sinh's yellow eyes turned a deep, sapphire blue, and his legs were suffused with a warm, brown-velvet tone, except for his feet, which remained sparkling white, a sign of the purity of Mun Ha's soul. Miraculously,

by the next morning, all the other cats in the temple had been transformed in a similar fashion.

For seven days Sinh remained at his post, guarding the fallen Mun-Ha. Then he died, carrying with him the soul of his master.

The French Connection

As one Birman breeder has observed somewhat laconically, "[the legend of Sinh] fails to explain the exact scientific origins of the Sacred Cat of Burma." Unfortunately, those scientific origins—as well as any exact accounts of the arrival of the first Birmans in Western Europe—are, as other cat writers are wont to say, "shrouded in mystery"—a shroud that is no less dense for being invoked so freely.

Feline history, for its part, records that the Birman's first toehold in Western Europe was established in France, where a pregnant female named Sita arrived in 1919. No one knows how Sita got to France, but there are three accounts—one virtuous, one venal, one problematic—that attempt to explain her presence there. In the virtuous account, Sita and a male named Maldapour, who died before reaching France, had been sent by a grateful priest to a British officer, Major Gordon Russell, who had helped several priests and their cats to escape from the temple of Lao-Tsun into Tibet during an uprising in Burma. In the venal account, "a certain Mr.

Vanderbilt" obtained two sacred cats (also named Maldapour and Sita) "for a price of gold" from a greedy servant who had stolen the cats from the temple. In the problematic account, included in the 1969 *Cat Fanciers' Association Yearbook*, one Verner E. Clum professed to have "a magazine dated 1927, *Le Monde Felin*, in which there is a picture of a Mme Marcelle Adam, first importer of [the Birman] breed in France in 1925." Mme Adam's cattery name, coincidentally, was Maldapour. She was president of the Fédération Féline Française.

Clum's account appeared to be the definitive version of Birman-importation history, but then Clum brought on that shroud of mystery in her next paragraph by recounting the Major Russell story without bothering to say which of the two individuals—Mme Adam or Major Russell—was, in her opinion at least, the first Birman importer. Interestingly, the pregnant Sita's fate is, by all accounts, unknown, but we are probably safe in assuming that her kittens, including a perfectly marked daughter named Poupée, were the foundation stock used to create the Birman breed in France.

The year 1925 is also important in Birman history because that is when Birmans were officially recognized in France, a fact that suggests Major Russell was the first Birman importer. Though it did not increase and multiply in biblical dimensions, the Birman prospered until World War II. The war had a near-ruinous effect on the cat fancy throughout much of Europe, and the Birman, like many other breeds, suffered a calamitous setback. At one point, a pair of Birmans was all that stood between the breed and extinction. Yet the Birman survived because of judicious outcrossing with other breeds, and by 1955 the breed was reestablished in France. Siamese and longhaired, bicolored Angoras are the likely participants in the Birman's resuscitation. It is fruitless, however, to theorize whether these cats—if they are, indeed, the ancestors of the modern-day Birmans—were conscripted intentionally for that purpose, or whether their contributions were simply the result of their interbreeding freely in an isolated setting. Whatever the breeds that came to the Birman's rescue, and however they might have joined forces, they had to have been carrying genes for point color, because the Birman's tail, face, and legs down to its feet are darker than the rest of its body. The collective ancestors of the modern-day Birman had to be carrying two other genes as well—a gene for long hair and a gene for low-grade white spotting. The effects of these genes, the particulars of which need not concern us here, are obvious. Which do you suppose is responsible for the Birman's coat length, and which is responsible for the Birman's white feet? Other than this, "L'origine des Birman est," as Hercule Poirot might have declared, "un mystère." (The origin of the Birmans is a mystery.)

Birmans in the United States

The first pair of Birmans arrived in the United States in 1959. By the mid-1960s, the breed began to be accepted for championship competition, and about that time its name was changed from the Sacred Cat of Burma to Burman, and finally to Birman.

The Birman Breed Standard

With the exception of household pets, all other cats and kittens that compete in a show are judged according to written standards for their breeds. A standard is like a blueprint that describes the ideal specimen in a breed. A standard is also like a constitution because it is drawn up by breeders, approved by cat-registering associations, and subject to amendment.

Pretty in pink or any other color. The person who could resist this kitten must be impervious to cute.

This kitten is attempting, with only limited success, to blend into its surroundings.

Each of the seven associations in North America that maintains registries and sanctions cat shows (see Useful Addresses and Literature, page 93) has its own set of breed standards. The differences among those standards are, for the most part, minor. In lieu of a tedious recitation of each Birman standard, we present here the following composite that draws upon the existing standards, incorporates the differences among them, and provides a good starting point for those seeking more specialized information about the breed.

Colors and Coat: To begin, the Birman is a colorpointed cat. Its face, tail, and legs, except for its feet, are darker than its body. Its silky hair is medium-long to long.

Conformation: A strongly built cat, the Birman is rectangular in shape and stocky in build. It is neither svelte like the Siamese, nor cobby like the Persian. Its tail is medium long, in pleasing proportion to its body.

Head: A Birman should have a strong, broad, rounded skull with a slight flat spot just in front of the ears, which should be medium in length and almost as wide at the base as they are tall. The ears should be modified to a rounded point at the tip, and should be set as much to the side as into the top of the head.

The Birman has a Roman (i.e., slightly convex) nose, medium in length and width. The nostrils should be set low on the nose leather. The backward-sloping forehead is also slightly convex. The muzzle is full and somewhat rounded; the chin is strong; the lower jaw forms a perpendicular line with the upper lip. The sweet expression that is characteristic of Birmans is due in great measure to their blue, nearly round eyes, which are set well apart and tilted just slightly upward at the outer corners.

Legs and Feet: The Birman's long (some cat associations say "medium-long") body is supported by medium-length, heavy-boned legs. The paws are accented by precisely defined white gloves, which occur on all four feet, and by aces, which are found only on the hind feet. The gloves on the front paws should end in an even line across the paw at or between the second or third joints. (The third joint is the place where the paw bends when the cat is standing.) The gloves should extend no farther than the metacarpal (dew) pad, which is located midway up the back of the front paw, above the third joint and just below the wrist bones. Symmetry of the front gloves, according to the breed standards, is desirable.

The gloves on the back paws should cover all the toes and may extend somewhat higher than the front gloves. Symmetry of the rear gloves is also desirable.

In addition to gloves, the Birman's back paws are decorated with laces, which are extensions of the gloves that stretch partway up the back of the hock. Again, in a perfect world or cat (which are the same to many breeders), the laces should end in a point or inverted "V" and extend one-half to three-quarters of the way up the hock. Lower or higher laces are acceptable, but in no case should they extend beyond the hock. Symmetry of the laces, too, is desirable.

Cats with perfect gloves and laces are rare. Whether or not breeders assert that divine intervention played any role in the origins of the Birman, they all acknowledge that divine intercession is needed to come up with perfectly defined white gloves and laces. Furthermore, one cannot easily predict which kittens in a litter will pass the white-gloves-and-laces test. "Birmans are born pure white," says one Birman breeder. "The color on the extremities comes in first. Then you wait for the gloves and laces to

"Standard, shmandard. It's what's inside a cat that matters."

appear. And you do a lot of praying." Which is how, come to think of it, the Birman story began.

Few breeds radiate innocence as well as Birmans do, and nobody does it better.

A Birman owner praying that at least one kitten will develop the correct markings.

Color Them Pointed

The following Birman colors are accepted for championship competition in all seven cat-registering associations in North America:

Blue point: The body is bluish white to pale ivory, shading gradually to almost white on stomach and chest. Points, except for gloves, should be deep blue. The gloves, of course, are pure white, the nose leather a slate color, and the paw pads, pink.

Chocolate point: The body is ivory and the points are a warm, milk-chocolate color. The nose leather is cinnamon pink and the paw pads, pink.

Lilac (or frost) point: The body is almost white and the points are frosty gray with a pinkish tone. The nose leather is lavender pink, and the paw pads, pink.

Seal point: The body is a warm, even, pale fawn to cream color, and the gloves are deep, seal brown. The nose leather is the same color as are the points, and the paw pads are pink.

Additional colors: The following colors, some of which are accepted in one or more of the six cat-registering associations other than the Cat Fanciers' Association, are too numerous to describe here. We shall, therefore, simply list them: red, cream, tortie, and lynx points; cinnamon, fawn, seal tortie, blue tortie, chocolate tortie, cinnamon tortie, and frost tortie points; seal, blue, chocolate, cinnamon, frost, fawn, red, and cream lynx points; and seal, blue, chocolate, cinnamon, frost, and fawn torbie points.

The Birman Buyer's Guide

The best place to buy a Birman kitten or adult is from a conscientious breeder with a spotless house and reputation who raises only two or three litters a year. (According to Cat Fanciers' Association statistics for 1993, three out of four breeders registered three or fewer litters that year.) Many breeders, conscientious and not so, advertise in cat magazines (see Useful Addresses and Literature, page 93). Some breeders also advertise in the classified sections of newspapers, on bulletin boards in veterinary offices, in grooming shops and feed stores, and in the yearbooks published by cat associations (see page 93). Prospective buyers also can meet Birman breeders at cat shows, which are advertised in newspapers, veterinarians' offices, the occasional pet store or supermarket, and cat magazines.

A Few Words about Cat Breeders

All breeders—and consequently all Birmans—are not created equal. Unfortunately, there are no intelligence or integrity tests required of those people who breed and sell cats. The phone number you obtain from an advertisement may lead you to a conscientious, compassionate individual motivated solely by the love of this breed and the desire to contribute to its ongoing perfection. However, you may also find yourself talking to a craven, opportunist who would sell a kitten to a band of devil worshipers as long as they paid with a certified check.

Sorting out the good, the bad, and the awful breeders is not difficult. If you approach a breeder's house and the odor makes your eyes begin to water as you near the front door, do an about-face and try another breeder. Conversely, if the breeder's place looks like the crew from *House Beautiful* are due any minute, and there is no evidence that a cat has ever set foot in any of its rooms, seek out a house that looks more cat-friendly.

The appearance of breeders and their houses is an important screening device in the cat-selection process. Even though temperament and good health are heritable to a greater or a lesser extent, the way a kitten is raised is usually more important in shaping its personality and in determining its state of health. Kittens that are not handled often enough between the ages of 3 and 14 weeks are less likely to develop into well-adjusted family members than are kittens that receive frequent handling and attention during this time. Therefore, it is important to ask how many litters a breeder produces each year and how many other litters he or she was raising when the kitten in which you are interested was born. A breeder who produces more than three or four litters a year—or who was raising two or three other litters while your kitten's litter was maturing—may not have had time to socialize every kitten in those litters properly. A breeder who raises only two or three litters a year—and

This Birman looks as if it was awakened in the middle of a sound sleep by a raucous party next door.

may require. Furthermore, persons buying a Birman from a breeder who lives beyond driving distance must pay to have the kitten shipped by plane. Shipping costs vary with the length of the flight, the method of shipping, and the airline involved. Kittens can be shipped on short flights for $30 to $40; transcontinental journeys can cost $100 or more.

The buyer also must pay for the carrier in which the kitten is shipped. Carriers that meet airline specifications can be purchased at cat shows, pet shops, or some airline cargo offices. A secure, durable carrier costs $25 to $35, depending on its size.

Getting Acquainted

When you meet your prospective kitten, you will naturally begin to size it up, and it will do the same to you. Little is known about the criteria kittens use to evaluate us "smooth tongues," but there are a few ways in which you can evaluate a kitten's personality.

To begin, simply wiggle a few fingers along the floor about 6 inches (15 cm) in front of the kitten, or wave a small toy back and forth about the same distance away. Does the kitten rush to investigate? Does it back away in fright? Or does it disappear under the nearest sofa? (The same test can be applied to adult cats, although their reactions will not always be as swift or as impetuous as a kitten's.) Well-adjusted, healthy kittens are curious about fingers, toys, and anything else that catches their eye. Nervous or timid kittens or those that are not feeling well are more cautious. Poorly adjusted kittens take cover under the nearest chair.

If you have other pets or children at home, the inquisitive, hey-look-me-over kitten is the best choice. The bashful kitten might well make a fine companion, too, but it may take longer to adjust, and is, perhaps, better left

preferably not at once—has more opportunity to give each of those kittens the individual attention it deserves. In general, the smaller the cattery, the more friendly the kittens it will produce and the more healthy those kittens will be.

How Much Is That Kitten?

The price of a kitten or cat is determined by quality, supply, demand, and geography. At this writing (spring, 1996), prices started at $300 to $400 for pet-quality Birmans, $500 to $600 for breeder-quality cats, and market price which begins at roughly $800 for show cats.

The purchase price is not the only cost associated with buying a kitten. New owners also have to pay for a veterinary inspection (a wise investment even though the kitten comes with a health certificate) and, perhaps, for any additional vaccinations the kitten for experienced cat owners who are currently without pets or young children. And the little one under the chair? Shy kittens need love also. Plenty of it. If you have no other pets, or if you plan to acquire two kittens at once and you have the time and patience required to nurture such a reluctant violet, the shy kitten will eventually repay your efforts. If you do not have the desire to work with a timid youngster, perhaps the next person who comes along will be the right owner for that kitten.

Signs of a Healthy Kitten
• A healthy kitten's eyes are bright, glistening, and clear.
• Its nose is cool and slightly damp.
• Its gums are neither pale nor inflamed.
• Its ears are free of wax or dirt.
• Its body is soft and smooth, perhaps a little lean, but not skinny.
• Its coat is shiny and free of bald patches, scabs, or tiny specks of black dirt.
• The area around its tail is free of dirt or discoloration.

A kitten with teary eyes may be in poor health, especially if its nose is dry or feels warm to the touch. Inflamed gums may indicate gingivitis; a kitten with pale gums may be anemic. If a kitten's ears are waxy inside, this may simply be a sign of neglect, but if they exhibit caked-on dirt, the kitten may have ear mites. If a kitten's ribs are sticking out or if it is pot-bellied, it may be undernourished or it may have worms. A kitten with a dull-looking coat or a coat dotted with scabs, tiny specks of dirt, or bald spots, may have ringworm, fungus, or fleas. A kitten with wet hindquarters may develop urine scalding; if they are dirty, it may have diarrhea. Both urine scalding and diarrhea are signs of potential poor health.

Finally, when you select a kitten, ask the breeder how that kitten behaves

The Birman personality, be it cautious or curious, is often revealed in a kitten's response to an invitation to play.

when being groomed, how frequently it has been groomed, and what sort of comb or brush the breeder uses with the kitten. If you go to the breeder's house to take delivery on your kitten, ask for a grooming demonstration (see Brushing Up on Grooming, beginning on page 33).

The Age of Consent
Cats are cats for many years, but they are kittens for only a few precious months, and new owners are understandably eager to take their kittens home as soon as possible. Nevertheless, responsible breeders do not let kittens go until they are at least 12 weeks old. By the time a kitten is 12 weeks old, it has been weaned properly, has been eating solid food for several weeks, and has begun to make the transition to adulthood. What is more, a 12-week-old kitten has had most, if not all, of its required vaccinations.

Kittens that are six to ten weeks old are still babies. If you take them away from their mothers and their siblings at that age, the stress of adjusting to new surroundings may cause them to

Read all contracts carefully before buying a kitten.

ing vaccine into a syringe and pushing the plunger. Few, if any, breeders are capable of examining kittens as thoroughly as a veterinarian can before administering vaccinations. This examination is important because a vaccine given to a sick kitten does more harm than good. Thus, a kitten should be seen by a veterinarian at least once before it is sold, preferably before its first vaccination. Finally, all kittens being shipped by air should be accompanied by a health certificate issued by a veterinarian, and by a certificate verifying that a kitten has received its rabies shot if it is required by the state in which the buyer resides.

become sick, to disregard their litter training, or to nurse on blankets or sofa cushions—a habit they sometimes maintain the rest of their lives. No matter how tempting an eight-week-old kitten might be, it will adjust better if it is allowed to remain in its original home until it is at least 12 weeks old.

Unfortunately, some breeders are eager to place kittens as quickly as possible, especially those breeders who have many kittens underfoot. Do not let an irresponsible breeder talk you into taking a kitten that is too young.

Papers and Health Certificates

The most important documents that accompany a kitten to its new home are health records and vaccination certificates. A kitten should not leave home without them, and a buyer should not accept a kitten without these papers. Some breeders, especially those that produce a large volume of kittens, like to save money by giving vaccinations themselves. There is nothing illegal about this, yet there is more to immunizing a kitten than draw-

The Sales Contract

Breeders should provide a sales contract soon after they agree to sell a kitten. Most contracts specify the price of the kitten, the amount of the deposit required to hold the kitten, if any, when the balance of the payment is due, and so on. Contracts may also specify that if at any time the buyer no longer can keep the kitten—or no longer wishes to keep it—the breeder must be given an opportunity to buy the kitten back at the going rate for kittens or cats at that time. (A contract specifying that the breeder be allowed to buy the kitten back at the original price would most likely not hold up if challenged.) Finally, a contract should specify that the new owner has a definite period of time, usually three to five working days, in which to take a kitten to a veterinarian for an examination. If the veterinarian discovers any preexisting conditions, such as leukemia or feline infectious peritonitis, the buyer should have the right to return the kitten at the seller's expense and to have the purchase price refunded.

Payment

If buyers give a breeder a deposit on a kitten, they should write "deposit for

_____ [the kitten's name]" on the memo line of the check. They should make a similar notation when writing a check for the balance of the payment. Buyers should be given receipts for all payments, and they should find out in advance—and in writing if they wish—whether a deposit is refundable if they decide not to take the kitten. Buyers also should remember that once a breeder has accepted money or some other consideration in return for reserving a kitten, they have entered into an option contract; and the breeder cannot legally revoke or renegotiate the offer, as some breeders may try to do, if the kitten turns out to be much better than the breeder had anticipated.

Buyers should read a contract meticulously before signing it because contracts are legally binding once they have been signed by both parties. If a contract contains any bizarre or intrusive stipulations that buyers do not understand or do not wish to accept, such as a stipulation saying that the breeder of the cat is entitled to come by and visit that cat on occasion, they should discuss these issues with the breeder before signing. Indeed, if the contract reads as if it has been written by a delusional law-and-order type with severe personality disorders, seek out another breeder.

Papers

In addition to the pedigree, new owners may receive "papers" when they buy a pedigreed cat. These papers usually consist of a registration slip that the new owners fill out and send, along with the appropriate registration fee ($6 or $7 at this writing, spring, 1996), to the administrative office of the association in which that kitten's litter has been registered. The association then returns a certificate of ownership to the new owners.

Persons buying a cat or kitten that already has been registered by its breeder will receive an owner's certificate. There is a transfer-of-ownership section on the back of that certificate that must be signed by the breeder and the new owner. Once the required signatures are in place, the new owner mails the certificate, with the appropriate transfer fee, to the administrative office of the association in which the cat has been registered. The association will send back a new, amended certificate of ownership to the new owner(s).

Many breeders do not supply a registration slip to anyone buying a pet-quality kitten until they receive proof that the kitten has been neutered or spayed, and some breeders do not supply registration slips on pet-quality kittens at all. Breeders withhold papers to prevent unethical persons from buying a kitten at a pet price and then breeding it, and to deter the use of pet-quality kittens in breeds that have virtually no chance of promoting the aesthetic advancement of a breed.

If You Want a Show Cat

Unless you are planning to show and breed, you want a pet-quality Birman. Pet-quality—an unfortunate and snobbish-sounding term—is used to designate cats with some cosmetic liability that argues against their breeding or showing success. Pet-quality Birmans may have ears that are set too high on their heads, white markings that are either too large or not large enough, or some other "fault" or minor constellation of faults. Such cosmetic "deficiencies" do not affect the kitten's ability to give and to receive affection, to knock the occasional knickknack off the shelf, or to live a long, contented life.

If you are interested in showing but not in breeding, you should look for a show-quality Birman. Many breeders are happy to sell show-quality kittens to persons who will allow the kittens the run of the house, have them altered

The chief counsel for the defense and his assistant listen to the judge's instructions.

Novices are at an even greater disadvantage evaluating a cat's show potential than they are when gauging its personality and general state of health. A runny eye is a runny eye to most observers, but eyes of the proper size, shape, and setting are more difficult for newcomers to identify; and the difficulty is compounded because kittens have yet to finish maturing.

That is why a journey of hundreds of dollars (or more) must begin with a few simple steps: Visit shows, talk to Birman breeders, watch Birman classes being judged, and learn what winning Birmans look like. Talk to judges when they have finished judging and ask them to recommend one or two Birman breeders, but do not put a judge on the spot by asking if the kittens from a certain cattery are good. If possible, visit several Birman breeders who are willing to spend an afternoon or evening "showing" their cats at home.

Most important, study the Birman breed standard (see page 7). Take a copy of the standard along when you go to look at kittens, and ask breeders to point out where a kitten or a cat meets the standard and where it does not. If the breeder does not object, take an experienced breeder along when you go to look at kittens.

Because breeders with the best available kittens will not always live within driving distance, you may have nothing more on which to base an informed decision than a few pictures and the breeder's evaluation. If the pictures are unclear, ask to see more. If you have any reason to doubt the breeder's word, find another breeder. In any case, ask the breeder to indicate, preferably in writing, where a kitten measures up to the standard and where it falls short. Breeders usually will not guarantee a kitten's performance in the show ring. As a Clint Eastwood character once said, "If you want a guarantee, buy a toaster," but a

when they are old enough, and show them in adult classes for altered cats.

If you are interested in eventually breeding and showing cats, you should start with the best quality female you can find. You should also remember that quality is not always proportionate to price and that registration papers merely indicate that a cat is eligible to be registered, not that it is good enough to be shown. Any registered cat can be entered in a show, but there is a qualitative difference between a cat that can be shown and a show cat. That difference, aesthetically, is akin to the difference between costume jewelry and a genuine pearl—often of great price.

Does the plural of couch potato end in s or es?

breeder should be willing to say if a kitten will be good enough after it matures to earn the titles offered by the various cat associations.

All in the Family

Anyone buying a show cat is also buying the constellation of genes that the cat has inherited from its ancestors.

17

The names and titles of the first four or five generations of ancestors are recorded on a cat's pedigree. Buyers should study a pedigree to see what titles the members of a kitten's family have won, especially its parents and grandparents, for the first two generations have the greatest impact on a kitten's appearance.

The most significant title awarded in the show ring is that of grand champion. The more grand champions present in the first two or three generations of a kitten's pedigree, the better its ancestors have done in competition, and the better its chances, theoretically at least, of carrying on the family tradition.

Although some kittens never look anything but promising from an early age, the average youngster goes through several stages while it is growing up—from ugly duckling to swan and sometimes vice versa. Buyers should wait, therefore, until a potential show-quality kitten is five or six months old before buying it. A five- or six-month-

Kittens need playmates. If you cannot afford to buy two Birmans, adopt a kitten from an animal shelter.

old kitten is less subject to change without notice than is a younger kitten. Buyers are wise to wait until a show kitten has reached that age, and, perhaps, has been shown a time or two.

One Cat or Two?

If you have no other pets and if your house is empty during the day, you should consider getting two kittens. If buying a second Birman kitten would fracture your budget, consider adopting a kitten—one that is roughly the same age as the Birman you are purchasing—from a local shelter. Not only are two kittens twice as much fun to watch when they are playing as one cat is, kittens are also less apt to be bored or lonely if they have another kitten to talk to when you are away. Of course, when you adopt a kitten from a shelter, you should follow the same guidelines you would follow when purchasing a kitten.

Fix Your Cat

Some people prefer male or female cats as pets, but members of either sex, if given love, attention, and someone to cuddle up with at night, make charming companions. The cost of spaying a female cat is one-third to one-half more than the cost of neutering a male. Neutered males, as they get older, should not be fed a diet with a mineral composition that would produce an alkaline rather than an acidic urine (see Nutrition and Diet, beginning on page 43). Otherwise, there is no difference in the cost associated with, or the care required in, housing an altered male or female.

The difference between living with an altered cat and an unaltered one, however, is not so slight. Unaltered cats are not as easy to live with as are altered cats. Whole males are wont to spray their urine to attract females and to regard any other cat as a potential mate or sparring partner. Females will come into season periodically, a condition accompanied by frequent caterwauling, restlessness, excessive attachment to their owners, occasional spraying of their urine, and an inclination to bolt out of doors within nanoseconds of their being opened.

In addition to the favor you will be doing yourself by altering your cat, you will also be doing a good turn for your cat's health. Unspayed females often develop pyometra, a severe uterine infection that is always debilitating and sometimes fatal. Spaying a cat before she goes into season for the first time (see The Female's Heat Cycle, page 75) may help to reduce (though not entirely eliminate) her chances of developing mammary cancer. Finally, spaying can help a female to avoid some varieties of skin disorders. Neutered male cats, for their part, are less likely to develop testicular cancer and other disorders to which whole males are prey.

The Pet-Store Kitten

Although it is unlikely, you may find a Birman kitten for sale in a pet store. If you buy that kitten, you will not—as virtually all breeders would declare—forfeit any chance you have for eternal salvation. You may, nevertheless, be buying a kitten in a poke if the pet store is unwilling or unable to provide the name, address, and phone number of the person who bred the kitten in which you are interested. If you cannot obtain that information, you should proceed with caution because you are making a decision with less information about the kitten than you

would have if you were buying it directly from its breeder. Moreover, many kittens for sale in pet shops are younger than 12 weeks old, which means they were taken away from their mothers too soon (see Age of Consent, page 13).

If the pet shop owner provides the name and address of the kitten's breeder—and if that person lives nearby—you should visit the breeder to observe the conditions in which the kitten was raised. If the breeder lives far away, you should telephone to ask questions about the kitten that the pet shop owner/manager might not be able to answer: How many other kittens were in the litter? How old was the kitten when it left its mother? How many cats does the breeder have? How many litters do those cats produce in a year? How many different breeds of kittens does the breeder produce? Why does the breeder choose to sell to pet shops rather than directly to the public? In addition, you should call the humane association in the town where the breeder lives to ask if the breeder enjoys a good reputation in that community. The humane society might not know the names of all the good breeders in town, but chances are the names of many of the bad ones will be available.

Recommending this sort of caution is not to insinuate that buying from a pet store is always more risky than buying directly from a breeder. What is implied is that you are entitled to find out as much as possible about a kitten's background, no matter where that kitten is acquired.

Making Your House a Home

According to Russian folk wisdom, a person bringing a new cat home should toss it onto the bed at once. If the cat settles there and begins to wash itself, it will stay in its new surroundings. If the cat dashes under the bed or out of the room, do not get rid of the cockatiel yet.

Perhaps some of the wisdom in this folktale was lost in translation, but the likelihood that a Birman or any other cat will approve of its new digs increases with the number and the kind of luxuries it finds there. Although cats, of necessity, have become adept at traveling light, they have never forgotten that once upon a dynasty, they

If a cat settles down after being tossed onto a bed by its new owners, says an old Russian proverb, the cat will remain in its new house.

were revered as gods in Egypt, and every cat, in its heart of royal hearts, is in the market for stately accommodations. So do not be fooled by a cat's hardiness. Any cat worth its heritage prefers the regal to the rustic, the palatial to the plain. Fortunately, a cat's idea of regal does not carry a heart-stopping price tag.

Shopping for Supplies

Certain items are necessary to make your Birman comfortable. Among them are the following:

Litter pan: Litters pans can be found in a variety of tints and configurations. Cats being limited in the apprehension of color, the choice of vermilion, egg shell, or azure remains with cat owners. To a lesser extent, so does the kind of litter pan used—open, enclosed, outfitted with a raised, detachable rim, or equipped with odor filters and opera windows. The filters are designed to take the worry out of unexpected guests. The window enables cat owners to determine—without having to lift the top off the pan—whether or not the pan needs cleaning. Enclosed pans and those with detachable rims are meant to keep the litter from scattering when the cat's feet hit the sand. No matter what style of litter pan you select, it should be at least 19 inches (48 cm) by 15 inches (38 cm) by 4 inches (10 cm) deep, and it should be made of sturdy, washable material.

Litter pan liners: These may not be practical for day-to-day use at home if cost and durability are considerations. Cats that dig too industriously may puncture the litter pan liner, and unless the trash can is right next to the litter pan, one is apt to leave a trail of litter from pan to can if the cat has poked holes in the liner. Liners can be convenient, however, for bundling up the contents of the pan and discarding them during motel stays.

Litter: Proceeds from the sale of cat litter account for more than one out of every three retail dollars spent on dog and cat supplies. With so much potential profit underfoot, it is not surprising that one of the giant pet-supply stores devotes 104 linear feet (31.7 m) to a display of 20 brands of litter. Among those brands, cat owners will find deodorant litter, superabsorbent litter, detergent litter, flushable litter, hypoallergenic litter, litter that clumps when it gets wet, litter that changes color to reflect changes in the pH of a cat's urine, litter that releases a fragrance in response to moisture or pressure, and litter conceived to work best when two or more cats use it. (How litter knows when it is being used by two or more cats is a question better left unpondered.) Litter is even available in materials other than the traditional clay, the principal ingredient of which is fuller's earth. "Nouvelle" recipes include litters made from recycled newspaper, ground corncobs, peanut shells, orange peels, pine sawdust, or rinsable pebbles. The manufacturers of litters made from recycled newspaper and corncobs claim that their products are more absorbent than are clay litters. Advertising claims notwithstanding, the cat owner should be guided by two principles when choosing litter. It should not smell worse than the material that will be deposited on it, and the cat should use it willingly.

Litter mats: Because litter is given to sticking between a cat's toes and to falling out around the house, several pet-supply manufacturers sell rubber pads that are purported to spread a cat's toes gently as soon as it steps out of the litter pan, thereby releasing any toe-jammed litter onto the pad.

Litter scoop: When litter scoops are the subject, beauty is as beauty does, and longevity is the most beautiful attribute of all. The sturdier the scoop, the better—and always have a spare on hand.

Food and water receptacles: Food dishes and water bowls should be made of glass, ceramic, or metal. Reusable plastic can retain odors even if it is washed carefully, and disposable plastic is an insult to the environment. Whatever their composition, all dishes and bowls should be solid and heavy enough not to tip over easily. Glass or ceramic bowls or dishes should be sturdy enough not to break, crack, or chip when a cat knocks them over or a human foot makes contact with them.

Ready for inspection: a spotless Birman, in a spotless pan, in spotless surroundings.

Place mats: Cats are normally tidy eaters, but the tidy owner may still want to shield the area of the floor or carpet on which food dishes and water bowls reside. A plain rubber mat or a glossy, vinyl, decorator model with unspeakably cute kittens cavorting on it will do the job nicely.

Scratching post: In theory, a scratching post spares the furniture while providing cats with a legitimate outlet for exercising their natural instinct to scratch. Some scratching posts are impregnated with catnip. Plain or scented, the post should be well anchored, so that it will not tip over when it is used, and it should be tall enough so that a mature cat can stretch while scratching. The scratching surface should be made of sisal or hemp or some other hardy, resilient material. Floor-to-ceiling scratching posts with shelves on which cats can sit and think—or merely sit—should be especially well anchored and secure.

The cat in the catbird seat on the top of the scratching post looks like the winner of a shopping spree in a pet-supply store.

Padded window perches: A padded window perch can transform a window with a narrow, cramped, and miserly sill into a plush, comfortable observation deck from which to threaten birds and to shout imprecations at the neighbor's cat. Most window perches can be clamped easily to the wall without advanced study in physics. Such perches can be obtained through a pet-supply catalog.

Grooming tools: Cats are naturally fastidious, and next to sleeping and eating, their favorite activity is primping. This meticulousness does not excuse cat owners from all responsibility for their cats' appearance. Supplementary, owner-supplied grooming should be part of all cats' routines (see Grooming Tools, page 34).

Toys: Cat owners can select from a dazzling assortment of toys, each contrived to afford a cat endless hours of fun. However, toys should be safe as well as seductive, and no matter how ingenious are the bells and whistles a toy might contain, safety should be the main criterion used in selecting toys for a cat. For instance: Balls with bells inside should be sturdy enough so that a kitten cannot dig the bell out and swallow it. Eyes, noses, and all appendages on small, stuffed mice and other prey substitutes should be virtually welded on for the same reason—as should streamers and any other attachments on toys.

Before buying a toy for your cat, imagine how that toy could cause harm. If there is any possibility that it could, it probably will. Do not buy it.

For all their fuss and feathers, store-bought toys are not the only games in town. Cats will derive enormous amusement from a crumpled piece of paper, an empty film canister, a cardboard box turned upside down with holes cut at either end, or a plain, brown paper grocery bag. (Indeed, some companies have built a better cat trap by manufacturing sacks that sound like paper bags when cats get to rattling around in them.)

The same cautions expressed about store-bought toys apply to the home-made kind:

• They should not be decorated with dangling strings for cats to get tangled up in or to swallow.

• They should not contain bits or pieces that cats can chew off and eat.

• They should not have sharp edges on which cats could get hurt.

• Cats should not be allowed to play with cellophane, plastic wrap, aluminum foil, twist ties from sandwich and garbage bags, rubber bands, or cotton swabs, all of which can cause them to choke.

Beds: Cats spend two-thirds of their lives asleep. A cat bed, therefore, should not be chosen casually. Nothing else you buy for a cat has the potential to be put to as much use. Cat beds are made in the image and likeness of hammocks, igloos, tents, paper bags, tunnels, and all manner of objects; but given even the most fanciful beds, cats often choose to sleep in a favorite window, on a comfortable chair, or on their owners' pillows. Before buying a bed for your Birman, you should wait until it has chosen a sleeping spot, then buy a bed to fit that spot and make it more comfortable. Fortunately, there are chair mats available if your cat insists on sleeping on an expensive chair.

Cat carrier: You will need a safe, sturdy carrier in which to bring your Birman home for the first time, to take it to the veterinarian's for checkups, and, perhaps, on vacation jaunts. A good carrier, besides having a secure handle and door latch, should be well ventilated and washable. Heavy-molded plastic carriers are the best choice. They can be purchased at pet shops, cat shows, and some airline cargo offices.

Food: Most supermarkets, pet shops, or feed stores carry a plentiful choice of foods to suit a cat's palate and nutritional needs. The food you select should provide 100 percent complete nutrition for the appropriate stage or for all stages of your cat's life—and should say so on the label. Products not meeting these requirements usually are identified as suitable for intermittent or supplemental use only (see Nutrition and Diet, beginning on page 43).

Home Is Where . . .

Cats are by nature predatory and possessed of a bristling sense of domain. In the wild—i.e., outside the house—cats lead singular lives consisting of low population densities, well-established rituals, limited interaction among adult cats, clearly defined territories, and one-tom-per-neighborhood leasing arrangements. Outside, every cat occupies its own territory, which consists of a home range and, contained within that, a smaller home area. According to one study conducted in London, England, the typical home range is about 0.3 to 1.2 miles (0.5 to 2 km) in diameter, depending on population density and location. The average home area is roughly 111 yards (101 m) in diameter.

The boundaries separating one cat's territory from another's are not precision etched. The home range of one cat frequently overlaps that of another cat, especially among males, which usually occupy larger home ranges than females do. For their part, however, females are more fierce than males in the defense of their territories, particularly their home areas.

Cats that live in overlapping territories avoid conflict by observing timetables for traveling through or staying in the commonly held portions of their domains. In addition, one cat may defer to another on sight, or after inspecting scent marks left on various trees and bushes along trails leading through the overlapping parts of their territories.

To virtually all pedigreed cats, Birmans included, the outdoors is something to pass through quickly in the carrier on the way to the veterinarian or to a cat show. Yet even though the Birman is many generations removed from anything resembling freedom, its instincts have not been fundamentally changed by its relatively brief tenure of domestication. Thus, like all other cats that are asked to spend their lives indoors in exchange for regular meals, human companionship, and climate-controlled lodging, the Birman is also obliged to adapt to conditions that violate the established patterns of life on the other side of the living room or cattery window.

Indoor cats rule much smaller territories than they would command outdoors. They meet fewer opportunities to exercise their natural instincts, and, in multicat households, they must tolerate greater interaction with other adult cats. These departures from a cat's natural lifestyle can lead to deviations in behavior, such as refusing to use the litter pan, quarreling with other

The behavior of cats that live indoors can be influenced by events they see outside their windows.

members of the feline brigade, turning the breakfront into a scratching post, and spraying urine on furniture, carpets, or walls. In fact, the more that indoor living stifles the expression of a cat's natural instincts, the greater the chance the cat will misbehave, if "misbehave" is the proper word. For what the cat owner sees as misbehaving, the cat no doubt sees as doing what comes naturally. A cat, after all, is an animal, not a miniature person in fur.

Welcoming the Newcomer

After you have bought every item on your shopping list, and a few extra toys as well, after you have washed the litter pan, filled it with 1½ to 2 inches (3.8–5 cm) of litter, and placed it in a quiet location away from places where your Birman is going to eat or to sleep, and after you have made a final safety check of the house, it is time to bring your new friend home. If you work during the week, schedule the homecoming ceremony for the start of a weekend or a holiday; and remember that even though you have planned carefully for this day, it will come as a world-class surprise to your Birman, who will be leaving its mother, playmates, and familiar people, and the only home it has ever known. Some kittens adjust swimmingly. After they are taken from their carriers and placed in their new litter pans, they look around as if to say, "Swell place. Got anything to eat?"

Other Birmans are not so self-assured. Do not be surprised or insulted if the newcomer looks apprehensive at first or looks around and scurries under the sofa. Sit down and have a cup of coffee, watch television, or read the newspaper. A calm atmosphere will have a calming effect on your cat, and eventually its curiosity will take over. No cat has ever refused permanently to come out from under a sofa. Once your cat has taken the measure of the underside of the chair, the newcomer will be ready to take the measure of additional parts of your house. You will have plenty of time to get acquainted then.

A cat will feel more comfortable in its new home if something from its former home is on hand—a favorite toy, a blanket or bed, a favored food, even a small amount of soiled litter from the cat's old pan to scatter in its new one. These items give off familiar, comforting smells that are reassuring in a new and potentially confounding world.

Litter Training

Although most kittens raised by their mothers, real or surrogate, are pretrained at the factory in the uses of a litter pan, there are several elementary principles of litter pan training with which cat owners should be familiar. As soon as you bring your Birman home, take it out of its carrier and place the cat in the litter pan. Always keep the pan in the same quiet, easy-to-reach place. While your new cat is getting used to its new surroundings, place it gently into the pan after meals, naps, and spirited play to reinforce its instincts. Praise your cat quietly after it has used the pan. Do not allow your cat to wander far from the litter pan room unless you are along to supervise. If you leave your cat home alone, confine it to the room in which the litter pan is located.

If Your Cat Misbehaves

If your cat makes a mistake, clean the spot with a nonammonia-based, disinfectant cleaner, then sprinkle a bit of white vinegar and salt on the spot to remove the odor. A cat's attention span is roughly 20 seconds. You will not be teaching it a lesson if you drag it to the scene of the crime and scold it. This will only teach the cat that humans behave strangely at times.

Should you catch your cat misbehaving, a stern, disapproving no will convey your displeasure. When your

A Birman kitten rises to the occasion when a feather toy flies into view.

cat is finished, carry it gently to the pan and place it inside to remind it that this is where to do its business. If accidents are repeated, perhaps the litter pan is too remote for your cat's convenience—there should be at least one pan on every story of the house to which a cat has access—or perhaps the pan is located too close to the places where your cat eats and sleeps.

"Flowers? What flowers? I wasn't going to eat any flowers."

HOW-TO:
Cat-proof Your House

Modify Your Cat's Environment

Because it is easier to modify a cat's environment in many cases than it is to modify a cat's behavior, the best way to keep cats out of mischief is to keep mischief out of cats' reach. The best-behaved cat is most often the cat with the fewest opportunities to misbehave. If you do not want Toby climbing up the draperies, you must provide him with something he can climb. If you do not want Ruffles scratching the sofa, you must provide her with something into which she can sink her claws. If you do not want Niles eating the houseplants, you must provide him with home-grown grasses for nibbling. In short, you must be creative enough to find ways of recapitulating a cat's natural world in an artificial indoor environment—providing toys that inspire hunting and chasing, cat "trees" that extend an opportunity to climb, secluded areas that furnish privacy, and windows that afford an opportunity to observe the world from which indoor cats are excluded. In addition, catnip for the occasional high, and comfortable beds for sleeping should all be part of the indoor cat's environment.

Eliminating Dangers

• If there are rooms you do not want your cat to investigate, keep the doors to those rooms closed.
• If there are fragile objects in the rooms your cat is allowed to visit, put them out of reach.
• Make sure all balconies are enclosed and all window screens are secured.
• See that all electrical cords are intact. If your cat or kitten begins teething on electrical cords, wrap them in heavy tape or cover them with plastic tubes, which you can buy in an auto supply shop. If necessary, unplug all appliances that are not in use until you are certain your cat has not developed a taste for electrical cords. To keep your cat from getting a charge out of electrical sockets, cover them with plastic, plug-in socket guards, which you can buy at the hardware store.

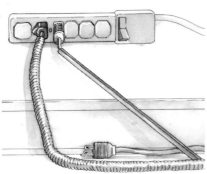

Electrical cords will be less electrifying for your cat if they are covered properly.

• Keep all kitchen and bathroom cleansers, chemicals, cleaners, and toilet articles in cabinets that can be closed or locked securely.
• Keep the lids on all trash receptacles tightly closed. Consider replacing trash containers whose swing-open lids could be dislodged if your cat overturns the containers. Another lid to keep down is the toilet seat lid.
• When closing any door in your house—the front door, back door, refrigerator door, closet door, the door on the clothes washer or dryer—be sure your cat is not on the wrong side. Keep the bathroom door closed when you are filling the tub.
• When cleaning, rinse all cleansers and chemicals thoroughly from any surfaces on which a cat could walk. What gets on a cat's paws usually winds up in its stomach.
• Put sewing supplies and yarn away when you are finished using them.
• Do not leave rubber bands, hot irons, cigarettes, plastic bags, or pieces of string or yarn lying around.

Learn to think like a cat. Look for any potential accident—tinsel on a Christmas tree, an overhanging tablecloth, a hot burner on the stove—waiting for a cat to make it happen.

Plants

Finally, keep poisonous plants out of reach. Many beautiful, harmless-looking plants are capable of producing illness or death in cats. Noxious plants can be grouped according to the effect they produce in animals: gastrointestinal, cardio-vascular, nervous system, and irritation or mechanical. The safest way to enjoy your cat and your plants, too, is by hanging the latter well out of the former's reach.

Plants with gastrointestinal effects: These include: amaryllis, azalea, bittersweet, bird of paradise, black locust, buckeye (horse chestnut), castor bean, common box, daffodil, daphne, English ivy, eggplant, euonymus, four-o'clock, ground cherry, holly, honeysuckle, hyacinth, iris (flag), jasmine, Jerusalem cherry, lords and ladies, mock orange, mushrooms, potato, privet, spurges, rain tree (monkeypod), rhododendron, sandbox tree, wisteria, yellow allamanda, yew.

Plants with cardiovascular effects: These include: anconite, foxglove, larkspur, lily of the valley, monkshood, oleander, yellow oleander, yew.

Plants with nervous system effects: These include: angel's trumpet, almond, apple, apricot,

Cats should be escorted from the bathroom when the tub is being filled, or is occupied.

belladonna, bleeding heart, cardinal flower, cherry, chinaberry tree, deadly nightshade, Dutchman's-breeches, elderberry, goldenrain tree, henbane, hydrangea, jasmine, jimsonweed, Kentucky coffee tree, lantana, marijuana, mescal bean, moonseed, morning glory, peach, periwinkle, thorn apple, tobacco, tree tobacco, yellow jasmine.

Plants that produce irritation or mechanical injury: These include: barleys, blackberry, bromegrasses, burdock, cacti, caladium, calla lily, Carolina nightshade, cocklebur, dumbcane, dieffenbachia, elephant's ear, foxtail, goathead, jack-in-the-pulpit, needlegrass, nettle, poinsettia, philodendron, pyracantha, sandbur, snow-on-the-mountain, spurge, triple awn.

Don't let your cat try this at home: a young Birman athlete navigating an obstacle course.

The cat's meow ranges from silent to basso profundo. Which do you suppose this is?

Disposing of Waste

Dirty pans can cause accidents. All waste should be scooped out of the pan and disposed of every day. Additional litter should be added as required. Once a week—or sooner if your nose suggests—dump all the litter, wash the pan thoroughly with a mild, nonammonia-based cleaner, rinse well, and put 1 to 2 inches (2.5 to 5 cm) of fresh litter in the pan.

Changing Litter

If your cat is comfortable with one kind of litter, stick with that brand (see page 21). Cats are creatures of habit as well as cleanliness. Switching litter may upset your cat's routine, which can result in accidents. If you must, for some reason, change to a new kind of litter, fold a small, unnoticeable amount of the new litter into the old kind at the weekly litter change. On successive weeks, fold increasing amounts of the new litter into the mix until the changeover has been effected.

Introducing Children

Before discussing how children need to be taught to respect cats and to handle them properly, we should sound a few cautions about buying kittens for children. To begin, parents should never buy a pet for their children "only if you promise that you're going to take care of it, or else I'll take it back." Children will make that promise faster than most guilty politicians will accept a plea bargain, but if the child reneges on that promise, Mom or Dad winds up taking care of the cat, and the child has learned the rewards of irresponsibility. Or if the parent makes good on the threat to get rid of the pet, the child learns that pets are disposable commodities, a lesson that is brought home all too often in this society.

Children cannot learn to take care of a cat until they have learned to treat it properly. Youngsters who are too immature to appreciate a cat can pose a threat to its sense of confidence and safety. Therefore, children who live with cats must be mature enough to understand that cats do not like to be disturbed when they are eating or sleeping or using their litter pans, that there is a right way to hold a cat, that cats are not toys to be lugged around the house, and that a litter pan is not a sandbox. For these reasons, parents with toddlers should wait until their children are roughly four years old before buying a cat or kitten.

Children do not always understand that what is fun for them may be painful for a cat. They must be careful to watch where they walk and run when the cat is around. Because cats often are frightened by loud, unfamiliar sounds, children must speak and play quietly until the cat gets used to them. Children must not pick the cat up until it is comfortable enough in its new surroundings not to be traumatized by an impromptu ride. Children should be taught the proper way to hold a cat: one hand under the cat's rib cage just behind the front legs, the other hand under the cat's bottom, with the cat's face pointing away from theirs. Have them practice this while sitting down in case they drop the cat or it jumps from their arms. Parents should reinforce their good advice with good example. If a parent disciplines a cat by striking it, their children will, too.

Cats can inspire a sense of responsibility in children, but children never should be forced to take care of animals. And even when a child is a cooperative caregiver, parents should keep an unobtrusive eye on the cat's feeding schedule, litter pan, and general condition. Parents should remember also that when they buy kittens for their youngsters, they buy the kittens for themselves. Inevitably, even the most cat-responsible teenagers grow up and leave home, and they do not always take their cats with them, especially when they go off to college.

Introducing Other Pets

You also should be cautious when introducing a Birman to other four-legged members of the family. The chances of hostilities breaking out vary inversely with the age and tenure of the cat or dog already in residence. If you have an eight-year-old pet that has always been an only child, you probably should not get a new cat or kitten. If your pet is four years old or younger, you should be able to introduce a new cat if you manage the introduction carefully—and if you keep in mind how you would feel if a stranger suddenly was brought to your house for an indefinite stay.

Again, bring the new cat home on a weekend or holiday. Before you do, prepare a room where the newcomer will spend some time in isolation. Do not

Children must be taught the proper way to handle a kitten.

select the old cat's favorite sanctuary or resting place for this purpose. The idea is to fit the new cat into the old cat's routine, not to make the old cat feel dethroned.

Solitary confinement is recommended for the new cat no matter how current the old cat's vaccinations are or how well the new cat passed its veterinary test. Until you are satisfied that the new cat is not harboring any contagions that did not show up during the veterinarian's inspection—that is, for ten days to two weeks—it should have no direct and prolonged contact with the old cat. Your new pet, of course, should have plenty of visits from you, and you should disinfect your hands thoroughly after each visit.

For the first few days, allow the cats to sniff, and perhaps to hiss, at each other from either side of a closed door. When you feel the time is right, and after you have clipped both cats' claws (see Clipping Your Birman's Claws, page 35), put the new cat into the cat carrier, open the door to the new cat's room, and allow the old cat to come in for a ten-minute visit. Be sure to take up the new cat's water bowl, food dish, and litter pan first in case the new cat is carrying an infectious disease.

Repeat these daily visits until any hissing, growling, or back arching subsides, then bring the old cat into the isolation ward, but do not confine the new cat beforehand. Put the old cat on the floor and retire to a neutral corner, but have a blanket, a broom, and a pan of cold water or a fully automatic water gun handy. If the rare, life-threatening fight erupts, use the pan of water, the water gun, and/or the broom to separate the cats, and throw the blanket over the nearest one. While the cat is wriggling around underneath the blanket, pick the cat up and return it to its original territory.

After a day or so, reinstate the brief visitations. A few days after that,

attempt the free-range introduction again. Do not fret if the cats refuse to curl up together. The best they may achieve is a distant but tolerant relationship that will allow them to coexist while you go about your normal routine.

Introducing Dogs

The rules for introducing a cat to a resident dog are much the same. Putting a lead on the dog will make separating them easier, if necessary. Do not remove the lead until you are sure the participants will not start fighting like cats and dogs. Be especially careful if you have a terrier, a sight hound, a retriever, or any dog that might consider the cat fair game.

Traveling with Your Cat

If your Birman complains all the way to the veterinarian or throws up and/or eliminates within five minutes from home, neither of you will enjoy a six-hour ride to your vacation retreat. There are pills, given about a half hour before departure, that will settle a cat's stomach, but its intestines are another matter. If you must travel with a nervous cat, always travel with a roll of paper towels, some small plastic bags, and a nonammonia-based spray cleanser. And never allow your cat to ride loose in the car or to remain in the car unattended, even for a few minutes.

For journeys of more than three or four hours, tape a small litter pan containing a small amount of litter to the floor inside the carrier. Cover the rest of the carrier floor with a towel or disposable diaper.

If there is room in your vehicle, your cat will be more comfortable in a small wire crate roughly 20 inches (51 cm) by 24 inches (61 cm) by 21 inches (53 cm) high. A crate this size will accommodate a small litter pan and will allow your cat to move around a bit. Drape a sheet or a towel over the crate to block the sun.

Air Travel

Air travel is even more challenging than car travel. Before jetting off to the Florida Keys, ask yourself why you want to take your cat along. To make you happier? Or to make the cat happier? If you cannot swear that your cat would gladly submit to round-trip air travel to be with you, then leave it home.

Cats can travel as carry-on luggage or excess baggage on commercial flights. As carry-on luggage, they ride in the cabin with their owners. Because most airlines allow only one in-cabin animal per flight, make reservations early.

In-cabin carriers must be small enough to fit under the passenger seat: roughly 17 inches (43 cm) long, 12 inches (30 cm) wide, and 8 inches (20 cm) high. If you want to find out how cramped that feels to a cat, and you happen to have a coffin around the house, punch some air holes in the side and spend a few hours in it, with the lid down. Mini-kennels, which are available from most airlines and pet shops, should be made of heavy-molded plastic and should meet airline specifications.

If someone else's pet claims the cabin space, your cat is excess baggage, in which case you will need a bigger kennel, one large enough to allow your cat to stand up and to turn around. Again, if the journey is more than three or four hours long, tape a small litter pan containing a small amount of litter to the floor inside the carrier. Cover the rest of the carrier floor with a towel or disposable diaper. To make this or any trip less stressful, put one of your cat's favorite blankets or toys in the carrier. Make sure the toy is something soft that you can secure to the inside of the kennel.

Pets shipped as excess baggage travel with the passengers' luggage in a part of the plane that is illuminated and maintained at the same pressurization and temperature as the passenger cabins. Because oxygen is limited in the hold, you will need to make reservations for this section, too. If possible, book a nonstop flight or find a direct flight so your cat does not have to be taken off one plane and put on another.

Airlines require that traveling pets arrive with health certificates issued by a veterinarian within the last 10 to 30 days. Some states require vaccinations, particularly rabies shots, as well. Whatever the regulations, your cat should have a preflight veterinary checkup. Some airlines suggest tranquilizing a cat before putting it on a plane. If your veterinarian agrees, fine.

Do not feed your cat within 12 hours of flight time, and make that meal a light one. A little chicken and rice are better than kibble or red meat. Also, do not give your cat too much water before the flight.

Leaving Your Cat at Home

Many people are wary about leaving their cats in a boarding kennel for fear they will be upset by the experience or will bring home fleas or something worse. A happy alternative is the pet sitter, who will feed, groom, medicate, and pet your cat, clean its litter pan, call the veterinarian in case of emergency, and, if necessary, tuck your cat into bed at night. Pet sitters also will bring in the mail and the newspaper, take out the trash, water the plants, and leave the television on overnight to create the impression that somebody other than Toby or Bowser is home. All this for a fee not much higher than the daily rate at a boarding kennel.

Most cats, especially older ones, will be happier if they can remain home while their owners are away. Though deprived of their owners' company, Birmans will still enjoy their favorite place to sleep, their arsenal

Summertime and the carrier is lightweight.

of toys, and their customary food. They will be surrounded by familiar household smells, and, most important, they will not be exposed to strange noises or smells that could upset them, or to other animals with fleas or contagious diseases.

Look in the Yellow Pages or ask your veterinarian where to locate a pet sitter. Perhaps a technician at the veterinarian's office would be willing to pet sit while you are away. You might even call a boarding kennel and ask if there is a pet sitter on staff.

Wherever you find one, be sure to interview the pet sitter in your home before you hand over the keys. Ask for and check references, and make sure the pet sitter is licensed, bonded, and insured. An interview gives you and your cat a chance to evaluate the pet sitter. What's more, the pet sitter will not be a total stranger the first time he or she arrives to care for your cat.

If there are no pet sitters in your area, choose a boarding kennel as if you were choosing a summer camp for the kids: Pay a surprise, midweek visit to the kennel and ask for a tour of the premises. Do not be shy about asking questions: Is the facility licensed? Is there a veterinarian on call around the clock? Who is the veterinarian and what is his or her phone number? Ask if your veterinarian would recommend the kennel. Finally, call the Better Business Bureau to ask if there are any complaints on file about the facility.

Brushing Up on Grooming

The cat owner who regards grooming as a chore will soon have a cat that feels the same way. Cats are thought by some people to be able to sense the faint quivering that foretells an earthquake days before it occurs. Be that as it may, a cat surely can interpret the look of distress on an owner's face or read the note of grief in an owner's voice if that owner would rather be doing something other than grooming the cat when it is time to do so.

Owners should approach grooming, therefore, with the same warm anticipation with which they would approach a visit from a treasured friend, for if your cat is not your treasured friend, who is? Grooming is an occasion to make your cat feel that it is the center of the universe. (Cats are inclined to believe that anyway, to be sure, but they never tire of hearing it.) Indeed, for the five minutes or so that you are grooming your cat, it is the world. Grooming always should be accompanied, then, by generous talking and purring, and in no time your cat will be purring, too. While you are grooming, listen to any complaints your cat might want to voice. Tell it your troubles and share your dreams with it. When you are finished with this soulful tête-à-tête, be sure to send your cat back to what it was doing with a joyous hug and, on occasion, an edible token of your affection.

The Logic of Grooming

In addition to deepening the bond between you and your Birman, grooming also gives you an opportunity to see what condition the cat is in. If your cat has been visited by fleas, grooming will alert you to their presence. If it has developed a rash or the beginnings of a mat in its coat, grooming will reveal it. If your cat has brought home ringworm from a show, grooming will tell the tale. Besides, the more hair you remove from your cat, the less it will swallow while grooming itself, and the fewer hairballs it will develop.

Grooming is also necessary because the Birman is a semilong-haired cat, and the longer a cat's fur, the more help it needs to keep it spiffy. Granted, the cat has earned a reputation for cleanliness, and next to sleeping, what a cat does most is fuss with its appearance. Moreover, nature has

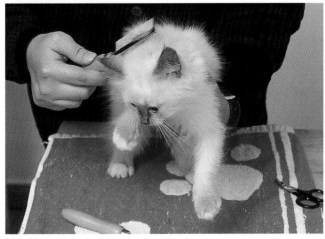

Handsome is as handsome is groomed.

equipped the cat with a brush for a tongue. The cat's tongue is, in fact, a pink, flexible rasp, dotted with tiny, prickly knobs called *papillae*. The filiform papillae in the center of the tongue are backward-facing hooks that the cat uses to polish its fur when not using them to hold food, to scrape bones clean, or to favor you with sandpapery kisses.

Nevertheless, even the most persnickety feline will hatch the occasional mat in a hard-to-reach place, and semilonghaired cats like the Birman, persnickety or otherwise, are distressingly prone to gathering debris in the pantaloons that decorate their hindquarters. Thus, you will have to develop a certain dexterity with comb and brush if your cat is going to stay bandbox clean.

Setting a Grooming Schedule

Like virtue, grooming is its own reward. The more dead hair you collect from your Birman, the less you have to collect from the furniture, the rugs, your clothing, or any food you drop on the floor—and the less likely you are to encounter a foul, oozing hairball while you are making your way to the bathroom in the middle of the night.

The need for grooming, as we have noted, increases in direct proportion to the length of a cat's coat. A shorthaired cat will remain glistening on one or two groomings a week, and shorthairs require infrequent bathing—if they require bathing at all. Some longhaired cats—the Persian and the Himalayan particularly—want three grooming sessions a week, perhaps more, and they should be bathed at least quarterly. The Birman's semilonghair coat will need more grooming than a shorthaired cat's but not as much as a Persian's or a Himalayan's because the Birman's silky coat is easier to groom and is less prone to matting.

A well-raised Birman kitten should not be a stranger to a comb or a brush, but if a kitten is not comfortable being groomed, remedial training should begin when that kitten has settled in its new surroundings. If you do not have a grooming table, and most cat owners do not, an ordinary table or a counter in the kitchen or the bathroom can serve as a grooming table—and so can your lap if you spread a towel over it. Avoid grooming your kitten on any surface, such as the kitchen table, where you do not ordinarily allow the cat to visit. If you remove your cat from the table one day, then groom the cat there the following day, you will be undoing the discipline you tried to establish the day before. You will also be confusing your cat. If there are no tables in the house on which the cat is allowed, perhaps you should visit a pet shop or a cat show to price grooming tables.

Grooming Tools

Grooming is the art of transforming a block of hair into a beautiful cat. Like every artist, you should have your tools ready before you begin working on your masterpiece. You will need all of the following tools some of the time and some of the following tools all of the time:

- comb(s) or brush(es)
- cotton swabs or cotton balls
- face cloth
- nail clippers
- lukewarm water
- rubbing alcohol
- mineral oil
- hydrogen peroxide
- a receptacle for dead hair

The tools you employ will be determined by the nature of the grooming session—a routine maintenance or a close-attention-to-details makeover.

Combs and Brushes

Once evolution had invented the opposable thumb, and human nature had invented vanity, it was only a matter of time before somebody invented combs. Once animals had been domesticated and the first animal show had been held (see Development of the Cat Fancy page 67), it was only a matter of time before somebody began using a comb to groom his or her pet.

Today, there are many pet combs from which the diligent owner can choose:

• A fine, all-purpose comb for grooming a Birman is one with ⅝-inch-long (1.6 cm) teeth that rotate as they move through a cat's coat. The rotating motion of the teeth helps to remove dead hair delicately. This kind of comb is available in 5- or 7-inch (13–18 cm) lengths.

• Another good comb for grooming a Birman has stationary teeth that are ⅞ inch (2.2 cm) long and are divided into two equal sections. The teeth occupying one half of the comb are almost 3⁄16 inch (0.5 cm) apart. The teeth occupying the other half are a little more than 1⁄16 inch (0.2 cm) apart.

• You will also need a flea comb. Beyond its obvious use, a flea comb is handy for grooming your cat's face and the areas between and behind the ears whether the cat has fleas or not.

• Some of the latest-model combs sport a Teflon finish that prevents the formation of a static charge, which makes grooming difficult when you brush your cat during the winter or any other time when the air is dry.

No matter what comb you choose, the ends of the teeth should be rounded, not pointed, or else they might inflict pain on your cat.

Brushes are available in various materials and shapes. The bristles on some brushes are made of animal hair; other brushes have bristles made of plastic or stainless steel. The tips of the latter often are covered with tiny, plastic balls. Some brushes have natural bristles on one side and stainless steel or synthetic bristles on the other.

Many people do not like nylon- or plastic-bristle brushes because they might damage a Birman's coat or generate static electricity. Another brush to avoid is the slicker brush sometimes used on breeds with short, close-lying coats. The same caveat regarding the teeth on a comb applies to the bristles on a brush: The tips of the bristles should not be so sharp as to inflict pain on your cat.

Clipping Your Birman's Claws

After the preliminary kissing and cooing, begin each grooming session by checking your cat's claws to see if they are approaching lethal sharpness. When you check your cat's claws, it should be facing away from you, either standing on a table or sitting on your lap. Lift one of its front legs so that the lower part of the leg rests in your upturned palm. Holding your cat's leg gently but securely between the heel of your thumb and the tips of your middle, ring, and little fingers, grasp the cat's foot between your thumb and forefinger. Press down on the cat's foot

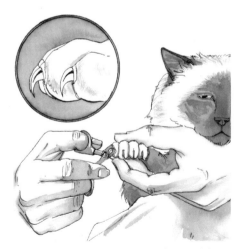

When clipping a Birman's claws, be careful not to cut into the quick—the visible, pink vein inside the nail.

with your thumb. This will cause the toes to spread and the claws to extend. Examine each claw individually. If the end is blunt or rounded, it does not need clipping. If the nail is honed to a daggerlike point, clip it. (You can buy a clipper for your cat's nails at a pet shop or a cat show or from a pet-supply company.) Be careful to clip the hooked part of the claw only. Avoid cutting into the quick, the pink vein that is visible inside the nail (see illustration).

Declawing: Bane or Benefit?

Rather than cope with the responsibility of clipping their cats' claws or contend with the possibility of their cats shredding the furniture, some cat owners simply have their cats' claws removed. This procedure, which is always performed under anesthesia, is properly known as *onychectomy*. Its popular name is declawing. When a cat is declawed, the entire last digit of each toe is amputated. This is tantamount to cutting off a person's finger at the last knuckle. Ordinarily, only the front claws are extracted, but some owners have the back claws removed, as well.

Critics of declawing raise a number of objections to this procedure: Putting a cat under anesthesia poses an unnecessary risk to the cat's life and health; the recovery from declawing can be painful and lengthy and may involve postoperative complications such as infection, hemorrhaging, and nail regrowth; declawing robs a cat of an essential means of movement and defense and, therefore, a declawed cat that is allowed outdoors is at the mercy of other animals; a declawed cat is often prevented from satisfying the instinctive impulses to climb and to chase, to exercise, and to mark territory by scratching.

Owners who choose to have their cats declawed maintain that the only other option was to place the cats in new homes. They also assert that declawing is a minor procedure that does not affect a cat's personality. If you are considering declawing, you must answer the following question: Would your cat be happier living somewhere else with its claws intact or would the cat be willing to sacrifice its claws for the pleasure of your company?

Combing and Brushing Techniques

Because many cats object to being groomed in some parts of their bodies—their bellies or their hindquarters, for example—do not take up the comb and head straightaway for one of these nonerogenous zones. Begin grooming, instead, at the back of the neck or the base of the spine. These are places that, upon being groomed, are virtually guaranteed to invoke purrs, simpering smiles, and backs arched in pleasure.

The Basic Method

Slide the comb into the coat at a 45-degree angle and comb with the lie of the coat at first. Do not push down constantly on the comb. Move it across the cat's body smoothly with your wrist locked. This technique also applies if you are using a brush, the only difference being that the bristles of a brush will meet the cat's coat at a 90-degree angle.

Young kittens and some older cats may need to be steadied—restrained, some might say—to receive the full benefit of your grooming attentions. If your cat suddenly remembers that it has a pressing engagement elsewhere the moment you begin to groom it, place your free hand on its chest while you comb its back and sides. When you are finished grooming those areas, place your free hand, palm up, on your cat's underbelly while you comb the hindquarters or neck.

To comb your cat's underbelly, place your free hand just behind and above the midpoint of the cat's front legs. Lift its legs gently until it is standing on its hind legs with its back at a 60-degree angle to the table. This technique is most effective if you and the cat are facing in the same direction.

Cats should be combed twice per grooming session, once to look for fleas, flea dirt, skin rashes, or mats in the coat, particularly in the armpits of the cat's legs and in the pantaloons on its hindquarters. If you find a flea and/or several grains of flea dirt on your cat, a flea bath is in order. If you find several fleas and/or considerable flea dirt, your veterinarian may recommend a more thorough campaign to rid your cat and your house of fleas. Skin rashes merit a visit to the veterinarian, who can assess the problem and prescribe treatment.

If you encounter a small mat about the size of a marble, do not try to rake it out with the comb or brush. Take the mat in both hands, instead, holding one half between the thumb and forefinger of your right hand and the other half between the thumb and forefinger of your left hand. Pull tenderly in opposite directions, being careful to pull parallel with your cat's skin. The mat should separate into two, smaller mats. Repeat the procedure, separating the two mats into four. The mats then may be small enough and loose enough to be tugged out carefully, one at a time, with the comb. If they are not, separate them once more and then comb them out.

Do not try to remove an overly large mat with the subdivide-and-conquer method just described. Instead, make an appointment with a groomer or a veterinarian and have the mat shaved off.

If you must try to remove a large mat, cut it with blunt scissors, leaving about ½ inch (1.3 cm) of mat. Do not try to cut

A face wash with a damp cotton ball often precedes a bath.

the mat any closer to the skin or you might wind up cutting your cat. You then may be able to subdivide the mat into small sections that can be teased out with a comb. (A mat picker, which can be purchased at most cat shows, can also be used to separate and to remove a mat from a Birman's coat.)

Cats are incapable of being wet and looking happy at the same time.

37

HOW-TO:
Bathing Your Birman

Most cat owners bathe their cats in the kitchen sink. A comfortable sink is at least 19 inches (48 cm) wide, 16 inches (41 cm) long, and 6.5 inches (17 cm) deep. The best cat-bathing sinks have built-in spray attachments. If yours does not, buy one at a hardware store, and do not forget to buy an adapter if you will need one to hook up the spray attachment to your faucet.

Because bathing a cat is an exercise best done with four hands instead of two, if someone in your family or one of your friends who is familiar with your cat owes you a favor, now is the time to collect. You also would be wise to have a cat carrier nearby with an absorbent towel covering its floor, in case your cat becomes unruly (or ballistic) during the bath and needs to collect its thoughts in private before you try again—or in case it needs to dry out before you release it for the day.

Prior to bathing your cat, lay out the tools you will need. These include:

- comb(s) or brush(es) or both
- two terrycloth washcloths
- regular or flea shampoo
- three bath towels
- cotton balls
- eight stacks of prefolded paper towels, about six panels thick
- blunt-tipped scissors
- toothbrush
- two small bowls of lukewarm water
- mineral oil in a squeeze bottle
- white vinegar (optional)
- mechanic's handsoap solution (optional)
- conditioning rinse (optional)
- hair dryer (optional)

Before putting your Birman into the sink, cover the bottom of the sink with a rubber mat or a bath towel to provide secure footing. Next, check your cat's claws. If they need clipping, clip them. Then check your cat's ears. After you have inspected the ears, and have cleaned them if necessary, put a small wad of cotton into each to prevent water from reaching the ear canal and possibly causing infection. Put a few drops of mineral oil into each of your cat's eyes to protect them from stray shampoo.

If your cat's face needs washing, clean it with lukewarm water and a washcloth. If the face is more than a little dirty, clean it with a weak solution of water and tearless shampoo. Squirt a few drops of shampoo into a bowl of lukewarm water, stir, and, using a washcloth, rub the solution carefully into the soiled areas on your cat's face. Rinse your cat's face by dipping a clean washcloth into a clean bowl of lukewarm water and rubbing the shampoo out of the fur.

Turn on the water and adjust the temperature, testing it with your wrist. If the water feels uncomfortably warm to you, chances are it will to your cat. Adjust the temperature accordingly. Make sure, too, that the house temperature is at least 72°F (22°C).

The moment of immersion is now at hand. Because prayer has not been outlawed in the home as yet, say a quick one and place your cat reverently into the sink. If you are using flea shampoo on your cat, wet its neck thoroughly at once and lather it well to prevent fleas on

Bathing a cat will proceed more smoothly if you gather the materials required for the ceremony beforehand.

38

the cat's body from escaping to its face. (Fleas are born with the knowledge that it is too difficult and dangerous to shampoo a cat's face.)

If your cat's tail or coat is greasy, take a handful of the mechanic's handsoap solution (available at hardware stores), rub it into the greasy spot, and work the solution into the coat. (To prepare the degreasing solution, combine half a can of hand soap with an equal amount of water and let stand overnight.)

After massaging the hand-soap solution into the greasy area, rinse completely. You are finished rinsing when the water coming off the cat is as clear as the water going onto the cat.

After you have degreased your cat, wet it down thoroughly with the spray attachment until the cat is soaked to the skin.

Then apply shampoo, lathering the coat generously. Never lather past the cat's neck no matter how badly any fleas on your cat's face are taunting you, or you risk getting shampoo into the cat's eyes. Put some shampoo on a toothbrush and brush the shampoo into the hair directly behind your cat's ears. If you use a regular shampoo, rinse your cat after lathering. If you use a flea shampoo, check the label first to see if the manufacturer recommends leaving the shampoo on the coat for any length of time before rinsing. (A flea bath is only part of the full-scale assault needed to rid your cat and your house of fleas, but space limitations prevent describing that campaign here. Consult your veterinarian or one of the summer issues of any cat magazine for advice about waging war on fleas.)

There are three secrets to a clean coat: rinse, rinse, and rinse. Some breeders use a pre-mixed vinegar-and-water solution as a final rinse for optimum soap scum removal. About half a cup of white vinegar in a gallon of water is sufficient. Other people prefer a conditioning rinse manufactured for pet or human use.

After your cat has been rinsed, take hold of its tail at the base with one hand, as if you were gripping a tennis racket, and squeeze gently, coaxing out as much water as you can. Repeat from midpoint to base of tail and on each leg. Blot your cat's legs, tail, and body with paper towels to absorb as much additional moisture as possible. Then remove the cat from the sink and wrap it in a towel, which can be warmed in the oven beforehand for your cat's postbath comfort.

A Birman pondering the mysteries of life. Or wondering why dinner is late.

strokes, or, with the cat facing the same direction you are, start behind the back legs and work toward the front in clockwise motions. A Birman's legs are combed or brushed downward with short strokes. For a show-ring appearance, you can comb or brush the legs upward to give them a fuller look.

The armpits should be combed with care because many cats are sensitive in those areas. To get a leg up on this job, lift your cat's leg and comb gently in the direction of the cat's body until the leg hairs have been separated. If your cat will tolerate the extra attention, comb once more, this time in the opposite direction.

To groom the tail, hold it gingerly by its tip. Beginning at the tip and working toward the base of the tail, move the comb or brush through the hair on the tail in short, incremental strokes, combing against the lie of the coat. (The cat's tail should look like a Christmas tree by the time you are through.) Then comb the tail again, but this time use the lift-and-flip technique, flicking your wrist in a counterclockwise motion as you work your way down the cat's tail from tip to base.

Comb the pantaloons in the direction that the fur grows first. Then, to fluff up the fur, comb the pantaloons in the opposite direction.

If your cat leaps off the table while being groomed, fetch the cat and return it to the table, even if you were almost finished. Retrieving your cat will be easier if you close the door(s) to the room before you begin grooming. After you have returned your cat to the grooming table, continue grooming. If you were nearly finished when your cat made its escape, groom for another minute or two anyway to let your cat know that grooming is not over until, as they say in sports, the fat lady sings—or until you say the grooming session is over.

Lift-and-Flip Technique

After you have combed your cat once, you should comb or brush him again. This time, instead of combing in long strokes in the direction that the coat lies, use a lift-and-flip motion to aerate the hairs. This technique will leave the cat's coat looking soft and glowing.

With the cat facing you, begin at the base of the tail and slide the comb or brush gently into the coat until you reach the skin. Then flick your wrist lightly in an upward, counterclockwise motion, lifting the hair against its natural lie. Continue backcombing the cat in this fashion until you have worked your way up to the head. Then run the comb or brush lightly through the just-combed portion of the cat to return the coat to its natural lie. Repeat this process down the cat's sides, working from the spine to the ends of the ribs.

A Birman's underbelly can be back-combed in either of two ways: With the cat facing you, start behind the front legs and work back in clockwise

Routine Ear Care

A few cotton swabs or cotton balls and some rubbing alcohol, mineral oil, or hydrogen peroxide in a small container are the only materials you need to clean your cat's ears. Dip the cotton swabs or cotton balls into the alcohol, oil, or peroxide (the choice is yours) and swab the visible parts of the ear carefully. Do not plunge the cotton swab or cotton ball down into the ear canal any further than the eye can see, or you might do some damage to your cat's sensitive hearing mechanism. If you wish to clean your cat's lower ear canal, buy a cleaning solution from your veterinarian and follow the instructions faithfully.

Drying Advice

If you want, you can allow your Birman to air dry after you have removed as much water as possible from its coat. Cats that are allowed to air dry, however, can end up looking like something the cat dragged in. Hair dryers are more efficient and produce better results. If you are going to use a hand-held dryer, put two or three drops of natural-tears solution or another moisturizing agent into your cat's eyes before you begin.

Cats do not take naturally to hair dryers any more than they take naturally to water. The best time to get your cat acclimated to the sound of a hair dryer is before you plan to use it. If you employ a hair dryer on your own hair, bring your cat into the bathroom or bedroom when you dry your hair. If you do not fancy the blow-dried look, run the hair dryer somewhere in the area where you feed your cat. Start the dryer on a low-speed setting before you begin preparing the cat's food. Leave the dryer running while the cat eats. If your cat shies at the sound, leave the dryer running and go out of the room for a few minutes. If your cat refuses to eat, take up the food, turn off the dryer,

Without the aid of a hair dryer a freshly bathed cat will end up looking like something the cat dragged in.

and try again in a half hour. Eventually, your pet will get hungry enough to eat with the dryer running.

Before using the hair dryer, put a towel on the surface the cat will occupy while being dried. Wrist test the temperature of the air coming out of the dryer. The air should not be too hot or too forceful. The best dryers are the ones with separate speed and temperature controls and quiet-running motors.

Some people begin the drying process by placing their cats in carriers with towel-lined floors. If you try this approach, position the dryer so that warm air blows temperately into the carrier through the front door.

After 20 minutes or so, take your cat out of the carrier and place the cat on a table or a counter. While directing a stream of warm air into the coat, comb cautiously. After the hairs in that area have been separated, move to another area of the cat. If you are attempting this job alone, be sure to use a hair dryer that has a stand into which you can set the dryer, thus leaving you with a free hand for lifting the cat while you dry and comb its underbelly. Be sure that the dryer stand is resting on a towel or else, as soon as you have the dryer adjusted to the proper angle for drying the cat's underbelly, the stand will start moving backward of its own accord.

When you have gone over the entire cat once with the dryer, begin again. This time, concentrate on one section of coat at a time. Do not concentrate more than a minute or two on any one section because the heat from the dryer could become uncomfortable for your cat. To avoid this possibility, keep the dryer moving back and forth above the section on which you are working.

As the coat becomes drier, use the lift-and-flip technique (see page 40) to aerate the hairs and to get them completely dry. Use a toothbrush (or a flea comb) to groom the cat's face. If you notice that static electricity is raising Cain with your cat's hair, rub a cling-free type antistatic cloth over its coat to smooth the hair into place.

If you are preparing your cat for a show, use blunt-tipped scissors to trim any stray hairs growing past the edges of the ears.

Nutrition and Diet

Cat food manufacturers spend serious time and money trying to reinvent the mouse. This all-natural, 100 percent nutritionally complete and balanced meal in the soft, gray, felt container provides the critical mixture of protein, vitamins, minerals, and essential fatty acids that a cat requires. Indeed, so perfect a source of nutrients is the mouse that one writer has asked—only half in jest—why "some enterprising company [does not] cook some mice, grind the little suckers up, and put 'em in a can?"

In lieu of such a parsimonious approach, cat food manufacturers keep redefining words like "nutritionally complete and balanced," and some set of government initials or other—currently the FDA (Food and Drug Administration), before that the NRC (National Research Council)—churns out nutritional profiles and guidelines periodically, specifying the maximums and minimums that govern the composition of cat food.

Fortunately, you need not take a home-study course in animal nutrition to feed your Birman a balanced, nourishing diet. In fact, you do not need to know a dispensable amino acid from an indispensable one, or the number of amino acids a cat requires, to be a good provider. All you need are a few fundamental coping strategies, which, of course, you will acquire by reading this chapter. Before we provide those strategies, however, we will present a brief discussion of the cardinal substances vital to a cat's well-being.

Dry, Semimoist, or Canned

Cat food is available in nearly 100 brands and three genre: dry, semimoist, and canned. Dry food is less expensive and more convenient to use than is canned food, and dry food helps to reduce dental tartar to some extent, an extent less prodigious than cat food manufacturers claim. Canned food, for its part, is more palatable than is dry food and, because canned food is three-quarters moisture, it is a better source of water than is other food. Semimoist food, because of its high chemical content, occupies a questionable, and not especially popular, middle ground between canned food and dry.

How to Interpret a Cat Food Label

Reading a cat food label is like squinting at the last line on an eye exam chart: You cannot be certain if you are seeing what you think you see, and even when you are certain, you are reading letters, not words—letters like *m-e-n-a-d-i-o-n-e s-o-d-i-u-m b-i-s-u-l-f-i-t-e*. These tongue twisters notwithstanding, the key statement on any cat food label is the following: "Moggy Menu provides complete and balanced nutrition for all stages of a cat's life, substantiated by testing performed in accordance with the procedure established by the Association of American Feed Control Officials (AAFCO)." Or words to that effect.

Let the buyer be aware, however, that all cat food is not suitable for all stages of a cat's life. Foods labeled "nutritionally complete and balanced

Despite their big words and small letters, cat food labels are not difficult to understand.

for growth and maintenance," or "for all stages of the cat's life," can be used from kittenhood through seniorhood, including motherhood. Foods labeled "complete and balanced for maintenance of the adult cat" would not be satisfactory for a kitten, a pregnant or lactating queen, or a cat with age- or disease-related dietary needs. (Cat foods that do not provide complete and balanced nutrition for any stage of a cat's life must be labeled as intermittent or supplemental foods only.)

Not every brand of cat food purporting to deliver complete and balanced nutrition was road tested in AAFCO-approved feeding trials. Therefore, some labels say, "Moggy Menu meets or exceeds the nutrient profiles established by the Association of American Feed Control Officials (AAFCO)." Or words to that effect.

What this statement does not say is that the food meets or exceeds AAFCO's nutritional levels before Moggy eats it. Whether it still does after the cat eats it is anybody's guess

because a certain amount of the vitamin and mineral content of food goes up in steam when food is cooked. For this reason, food whose nutritional performance has been established in feeding trials is preferred to food whose nutritional content is guaranteed to meet or to exceed AAFCO recommendations only at the predigestion stage.

How Much and When to Feed

A cat with constant access to food will eat as the spirit moves it, consuming several small meals a day rather than following a precise feeding pattern. Yet, even though cats prefer 'round-the-clock noshing (feral cats, too, eat several small rodent-cuisine meals each day), adult cats will adapt to being fed just once every 24 hours. Because adult cats are so adaptable, feed at a time that is convenient for you. Some people feed "wet" food, either canned or homemade, twice a day. Others feed wet food once daily. Some feed wet food once a day and always leave dry food available for their cats. Some people, and many laboratories, feed dry food only.

Kittens are not as feeding-flexible as adult cats are. When kittens are being weaned, starting at three to four weeks of age, they should be fed three or four times a day. Reduce feedings to twice a day at six months, and, if you desire, to once a day after a cat's first birthday.

Kittens also need relatively more food than adult cats require (see chart on page 45).

As the chart indicates, a ten-week-old kitten weighing 2.5 pounds (1 kg) would satisfy its daily food requirements by consuming 2.75 ounces (78 g) of dry food or 3.5 ounces (99 g) of semimoist food or 9 ounces (255 g) of canned food a day. A 10-pound (4.5 kg) inactive, adult cat would satisfy its daily food requirements by consuming

Two Birman adolescents holding a summit conference over lunch.

3.5 (99 g) ounces of dry food or 4 ounces (115 g) of semimoist food or 12 ounces (340 g) of canned food a day. These amounts may be lower than those specified in the feeding instructions on the cat food package. Food labels usually underrepresent the contents of the package, and they generally overstate the amount of food a cat needs.

Recommended feeding amounts are estimates based on data collected from many cat-feeding trials. A cat's metabolism, influenced by age and activity level, regulates food consump-

tion. One 10-pound (4.5 kg) cat might need half a cup of dry food each day, whereas another might need two-thirds of a cup. Pregnant and lactating cats will need more food than will other cats.

Before deciding what to feed your new Birman, find out what it has been eating. If its diet has been sound, continue with that product or products. Should you need to switch foods, which may happen if you buy a kitten raised on a homemade diet, mix new food with the old in a three-parts-old-to-one-part-new ratio. Every three or

Daily Feeding Guidelines*

		Dry	Semimoist	Canned
		(ounces per pound of body weight)		
Kittens:	10 weeks	1.1 oz.	1.4 oz.	3.6 oz.
	20 weeks	.6	.7	1.8
	30 weeks	.45	.6	1.4
	40 weeks	.36	.4	1.2
Adults:	Inactive	.32	.4	1.0
	Active	.36	.4	1.2
	Pregnant	.45	.6	1.4
	Lactating	1.00	1.3	3.3

*Adapted from *Nutrient Requirements of Cats,* National Research Council, 1986.

45

four days increase the new food while decreasing the old until the changeover is complete.

Though cats prefer their food at room temperature, they are not the notoriously finicky eaters that advertisers claim they are. Indeed, finicky eaters are made, not born. Two sure-fire ways to create a finicky cat are by feeding it the same food all the time or by feeding it people food. Give your cat a variety of foods and brands instead—meat and poultry for the most part, with fish for occasional diversity. And lay off the people treats, especially at the table. This is not cute, nor is it necessary for your cat's development or for civilized dining.

Are Supplements Necessary?

If commercial cat food is labeled "nutritionally complete and balanced," do not add vitamins or supplements to it, even when a cat is pregnant. Supplementary vitamins will probably upset the balance of vitamins already in a cat's food and may cause vitamin toxicity. The only cats that need vitamin supplements are those not eating properly because of illness, or those losing increased amounts of body fluids because of diarrhea or increased urination.

Clean, fresh water is indispensable to a cat's well-being.

Because mineral requirements are interrelated, the same warning about vitamin supplements applies to mineral supplements: Proceed with caution and your veterinarian's recommendation, if at all.

Liquids

Water is the most important nutrient required to sustain normal cell function. Mammals can lose nearly all their reserves of glycogen and fat, half their protein stores, and 40 percent of their body weight and still survive. The cat, composed of nearly 70 percent water, is in severe metabolic disarray if it loses 10 percent of its body water. Death results if water loss rises to 15 percent. Fortunately for the preservation of their species, cats can conserve water by concentrating their urine.

Water intake is primarily affected by diet. Because canned food is 75 percent water, cats fed canned food exclusively will drink less than cats on a combination canned-dry diet or a dry diet only. Whatever the case, give your Birman fresh water in a freshly cleaned bowl every day.

Although cats are terminally dependent upon water, they have no need of milk beyond kittenhood. As cats mature, they often become deficient in lactase, the enzyme that breaks down lactose in milk. Thus, many adult cats develop diarrhea from drinking milk.

Overweight and Underweight Cats

Cats gain and lose weight in cycles that may last several months. A cat is overweight if its abdomen begins to droop, if you cannot feel its rib cage when you run your hands along its sides, if it sways from side to side when it walks, or if it develops bulges on either side of the point where the tail joins the body. You can prevent these symptoms from developing if you weigh your cat once a month and act accordingly.

Whenever your Birman gains a pound, you should schedule an appointment with your veterinarian to determine whether that gain is the result of illness, especially if your cat has been acting listless or exhibiting any other signs of poor health (see Troublesome Signs, page 49). If you are satisfied that your Birman has gained its weight the old-fashioned way, by taking in more calories than it burns, reduce its food by 20 percent. The easiest way to monitor food intake is to feed your cat twice a day and to take up its food after 20 or 30 minutes. If you have several cats and you want to put one on a diet, you may have to feed that cat separately. This is easier said than done, but it should be done if you have the best interests of that cat at heart.

There is more than one way to thin a cat. Diet cat food, usually called "lite," allows you to feed the same amount of food while lowering a cat's caloric intake. Lite food contains 20 to 33 percent fewer calories than regular food. Lite and other special-diet foods should be fed only to those overweight, ill, or geriatric cats whose veterinarians recommend them.

A Breakthrough in Labeling

One weighty piece of nutritional information that should be present on cat food labels by the time this book is published (fall, 1996) is the food's caloric content. Previously, the cost of monitoring caloric claims prohibited states from allowing manufacturers to state caloric content. But in 1992, AAFCO accepted a procedure designed by its feline nutrition expert (FNE) subcommittee that allows states to verify by laboratory analysis the caloric-content claims made by manufacturers for their products. In early August 1993, the CNE's recommenda-tion was approved and was passed into regulation.

"Caloric-content information is probably more important than the current information on pet food labels," says one member of the CNE subcommittee. "Knowing the caloric content will enable consumers to make informed comparisons between products because consumers will have a meaningful way of determining that it is possible to feed X amount of this product and get the same effect as feeding X amount of another product."

Is Home Cooking Better?

For many people, feeding their cats is a sacramental experience involving Zenlike preparation and adherence to detail. Most home cookers insist that their cats would not be as healthy, sparkling, stress-resistant, and economical to feed on a commercial diet. They have the economical part right.

Foods to Avoid
- Table scraps: Not nutritionally balanced.
- Raw meat: May contain parasites.
- Raw fish: May contain parasites; may cause thiamine deficiency.
- Raw egg whites: Contain a protein that interacts with biotin, rendering it unavailable to the body. Biotin deficiency can cause dried secretions around the eyes, nose, and mouth, and scaly skin.
- Raw liver: Contains an excess of vitamin A and could result in vitamin A toxicity.
- Bones: May lodge in a cat's throat or pierce the stomach or intestinal wall.
- Dog food: Does not contain enough protein.
- Canned tuna for humans: Causes vitamin E deficiency.
- Chocolate: Can diminish the flow of blood and cause heart attacks.

Birmans have no bad angles. Each vantage reveals a masterpiece.

Ground meat bought from a pet food provisioner is much less expensive than anything that comes in a box, pouch, or can. But whether raw meat, sometimes cooked and always infused with vitamins, minerals, oils, and other molecular talismans, is better than commercial food is questionable. Anyone feeding cats a diet based on raw meat must add the right vitamins and minerals in the right proportions. This is more complex than pouring calcium, a few tablespoons of vitamins, and some brewer's yeast into the meat and mixing thoroughly. How much calcium must you add to raw meat, which is calcium deficient, to restore the calcium-phosphorus ratio to its optimal 1:1 to 1:2 range? How do you convert the 10,000 units of vitamin X per pound listed on the label of a 20-ounce (570 g) jar of cat vitamins into the proper amount that should be added to a pound of raw meat? Which vitamin additive is the most balanced and complete? Does it also contain the proper minerals in the proper amounts and ratios? And should you cook the meat or feed it raw?

Unless you have some special intuition or knowledge that cat food manufacturers with their million dollar budgets and their battalions of feeding-trial cats have overlooked, you should leave the nutritional driving to commercial pet foods.

A Realistic Health Care Plan

Despite their inclination to spend prodigious amounts of time in sleep— as many as 14 to 18 hours a day— healthy cats are otherwise active and alert. They display affection for their owners, concern for their appearance, and a keen interest in life, mealtimes, and their surroundings, though not invariably in that order.

Troublesome Signs

Often the first indication that a cat is not feeling chipper is a resolute lack of interest in food. *Resolute* does not mean a single missed meal. This is not cause for worry, but if a cat misses two consecutive meals, caution dictates a trip, or at least a call, to a veterinarian, especially if the cat's temperature is elevated or it exhibits any other sign(s) of illness.

Many symptoms are troublesome enough, however, to warrant an immediate trip to the veterinarian, as soon as you have called to describe your cat's problem and to request the earliest possible appointment. The following list presents some of those grave symptoms. The list is not intended to be used as a diagnostic tool, nor should it be considered exhaustive. Think of it, instead, as a genteel replacement for the tedious recitations of feline diseases that appear in many cat books. When a cat is ailing, the diligent owner does not need to speculate about the possible reason. The owner simply needs to know that certain symptoms warrant a call to the veterinarian.

Take your Birman to the veterinarian at once if the cat:
• has a temperature higher than 105°F (40.6°C);
• has a runny nose accompanied by a temperature above 103.5°F (39.5°C), pale gums, or weakness;
• breathes with difficulty after chewing on a plant (or at any other time);
• seems drowsy after eating a foreign substance;
• has a deep wound or a wound that still bleeds after you have applied pressure to it;
• displays any evidence of trauma accompanied by shortness of breath, a temperature of 103.5°F (39.5°C) or higher, pale gums, or lethargy;
• exhibits a sudden weakness in the hind end that makes walking difficult;
• has a red, ulcerated sore on the lips or any other part of the body;
• develops an abscess that is warm and painful to the touch;
• vomits and appears lethargic, attempts to urinate frequently, and has a temperature of 103.5°F (39.5°C) or higher, and/or bloody stools;
• has diarrhea, bloody feces, an elevated temperature, or is vomiting;
• is constipated and strains at the stool while failing to defecate.

Call your veterinarian for advice and an appointment if your Birman:
• has abnormally thin or watery stools and an elevated temperature;
• has a temperature between 103.5° and 105°F (39.5–40.6°C) and other signs of illness;

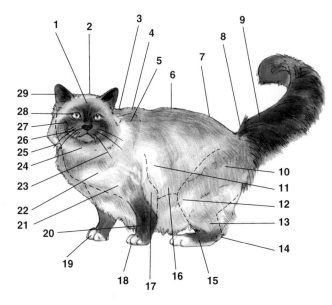

The external anatomy of the Birman.

1. Forehead
2. Crown
3. Neck
4. Shoulder
5. Shoulder
6. Back
7. Rump
8. Base of tail
9. Tail
10. Upper thigh
11. Rib cage
12. Knee joint
13. Lower thigh
14. Hock
15. Metatarsus
16. Belly
17. Elbow joint
18. Pad
19. Metacarpus
20. Lower arm
21. Upper arm
22. Chest
23. Whisker
24. Throat
25. Nape
26. Nose
27. Cheek
28. Eye
29. Ear

• begins drinking more water than usual and urinating excessively, has diarrhea, is lethargic, or has an elevated temperature;
• has a decreased appetite and is coughing, vomiting, or has diarrhea;
• exhibits general lameness in any leg for more than two days;
• develops a swelling that is warm and painful to the touch;
• has a runny nose accompanied by lethargy, pus in the eye, or rapid breathing;
• has a cough accompanied by an elevated temperature, difficulty breathing, and lack of energy;
• has foul-smelling breath, drinks water excessively, eats frequently, urinates frequently, yet appears lethargic;
• has diarrhea accompanied by dehydration. (A cat is dehydrated if you take a pinch of skin from over its spine between your thumb and forefinger, lift the skin away from the body, let go of the skin, and it does not spring back into place immediately.)

Preventive Health Care

Preventive health care, which begins with a trip to the veterinarian to have your Birman examined as soon as you acquire it, should include an annual visit to the veterinarian for a thorough physical examination, booster shots, and fecal examination, in which a stool sample is assayed to see if the cat is infected with certain varieties of worms (see Internal Parasites, page 52).

The Importance of Vaccinations

Vaccines against certain viral diseases should be administered in the correct doses by a veterinarian to a pre-examined, healthy kitten in a timely and proper manner. Nevertheless, when it leaves the veterinarian's office, a kitten is little different than it was half an hour before, except for a small quantity of vaccine that has begun to work its way through the kitten's body. Not for five to ten days will a kitten's immune system start to forge a response to the challenge posed by that vaccine. What is more, the response to the vaccine is low-grade and not entirely effective. A second and sometimes a third vaccination, each delivered at four-week intervals, are needed to incite more vigorous responses and to achieve peak immunization.

Vaccination, strictly defined, is the introduction to the bloodstream of a vaccine designed to protect against one or more afflictions. Immunization, the desired end product of vaccination, is the process by which disease-killing cells and antibodies are produced in the body's immune system. Thus, if a kitten that has been vaccinated against rhinotracheitis (an upper respiratory disease) is subsequently invaded by a rhinotracheitis virus that infects some of its cells, the kitten's disease-killing cells will recognize that virus and destroy the infected cells. Meanwhile, antibodies in the kitten's bloodstream will be on the alert for any rhinotracheitis particles circulating in the body. When such particles are found, antibodies lock onto them, and the particles are eliminated from the body after being engulfed by other cells that specialize in destroying harmful antigens (an antigen is a substance that stimulates the production of antibodies).

Newborn animals cannot produce antibodies efficiently because their lymphoid tissues do not operate at full strength. During gestation, kittens inherit immunity from their mothers, if they have antibodies in their bloodstreams. Thereafter, kittens are protected by antibodies in their mothers' milk until the kittens are roughly eight weeks old. This passive immunity interferes with kittens' ability to produce antibodies; therefore, they are not vaccinated for the first time until they are six to eight weeks old. Typically, a kitten is vaccinated against panleukopenia, rhinotracheitis, calicivirus, and chlamydia. The antigens representing these diseases are usually administered in a single vaccine.

Fewer than one percent of healthy kittens vaccinated at the proper age with the right dose of a properly stored vaccine will fail to produce an immune response. Like failure to develop immunity, severe allergic reactions to vaccination are rare. If they occur, the kitten should be taken back to the veterinarian at once. It is a good idea, therefore, to schedule vaccinations for early in the day so that if you have to rush a kitten back to the veterinarian, the office will be still open.

Some cats develop a small lump on their bodies at the site where they were injected. This lump is the result of a reaction to one of the elements in a vaccine. If the lump does not subside within a few weeks, or if it appears to bother your cat, call the veterinarian.

Next to the vaccine, the most important factor in developing immunization is the veterinarian, who by training and

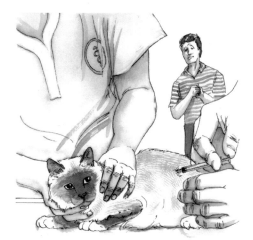

Vaccinations stimulate the cat's immune system to produce the antibodies needed to fight disease.

experience is best qualified to judge when a kitten is healthy enough to be vaccinated. For this reason, anyone buying a kitten from breeders who give their own shots ought to insist that the kitten be examined by a veterinarian before the first vaccination is administered. A vaccination is only as good as the exam that preceded it.

A Vaccination Schedule

The following comprehensive vaccination schedule is presented as a guide for new (and old) cat owners.

Fleas, Ticks, Mites, et al.

Parasites are living organisms that reside in or on other living organisms (called hosts), feeding on blood, lymph cells, or tissue. Parasites that dwell inside their hosts are called internal parasites (or endoparasites). Those that prowl on the surface of their hosts are called external parasites (or ectoparasites).

The cat's external parasites include fleas, ticks, flies, lice, larvae, and mites. In addition to damaging skin tissue, this motley collection of insects and

Age of Kitten	Type of vaccination
8 weeks	FVRCP—panleukopenia, rhinotracheitis, calicivirus, and chlamydia
12 weeks	FVRCP booster shot
	FeLV—feline leukemia
16 weeks	FeLV booster
	FVRCP booster (if recommended by veterinarian)
6 months	rabies
14 months	FVRCP booster, administered annually from this date— or more frequently if the veterinarian recommends
	FeLV booster, administered annually from this date
18 months	rabies booster, administered every one to three years from this date, depending on local vaccination requirements

Some cat owners also have their cats vaccinated against feline infectious peritonitis (FIP). The FIP vaccine is administered intranasally when a kitten is 16 weeks old. Booster vaccines are given at 19 weeks and annually thereafter.

arachnids may transmit harmful bacteria and menacing viruses to their hosts. In significant quantities, external parasites can leave their hosts devoid of energy, weaken their resistance to infection and disease, and infect them with a number of diseases or parasitic worms.

The presence of external parasites is usually revealed by skin lesions, hair loss, itching, redness, dandruff, scaling, growths of thickened skin, or an unpleasant odor. If any of these symptoms appears, take your cat to the veterinarian for a diagnosis. Cats infected with mites most likely will have to be isolated from other cats and treated with parasiticidal dips, powders, ointments, and shampoos.

Internal Parasites

Most cats are infected at one time or another with internal parasites. Some cats are born with them, having taken in worm larvae in their mothers' milk; other cats acquire them later in life. The four types of internal parasites that thrive in the cat are nematodes, cestodes, trematodes, and protozoa.

Nematodes include roundworms, hookworms, and threadworms. Roundworms, which live in a cat's stomach or intestine, can grow to a length of 3 to 5 inches (7.6–13 cm). The eggs produced by female roundworms are passed in the feces. Several weeks later infective larvae develop in the eggs. Cats that eat the eggs or that eat rodents with infective larvae in their tissues in turn become infected. As cats mature, they develop a resistance to roundworm infection. Kittens are not so fortunate, and a serious roundworm infestation can kill them.

The presence of roundworms can be detected by a veterinarian through stool sample analysis, and there are several medications that will rid a cat of these worms. The medications are not effective against dormant larvae, which can be resuscitated by immunosuppressive drugs, pregnancy, trauma, surgery, severe disease, and emotional upset.

Hookworms, ¼ to ½ inch (6.4–13 cm) long, live in the cat's small intestine. Known for their longevity, hookworms are thought to be capable of living the entire life span of a cat. Cats can become infected with hookworms after ingesting contaminated soil or after hookworm larvae have penetrated their skin. Kittens can take in hookworm larvae while nursing. Hookworms can cause anemia in cats and death from anemia in kittens. The presence of hookworms can be detected through stool sample analysis, and they can be eliminated with deworming medication.

Threadworms, ⅛ to ⅕ of an inch (3.2–5.1 mm) in length, also live in the cat's intestine. Threadworm eggs are passed in feces. The larvae that develop in them gain entrance to a cat by penetrating its skin. The presence of threadworms can be detected by stool sample analysis; they have been eliminated successfully by some drugs.

Cestodes (or tapeworms) are the most common internal parasite of the adult cat. The scolex (head) of the tapeworm fastens itself to the wall of the gut by hooks and suckers. The body, which can vary in length from less than an inch (2.5 cm) to several feet (31 cm per foot), is composed of segments that contain egg packets. These segments are shed in a cat's feces, where they are quite disgustingly—but fortunately—visible, because tapeworms are not amenable to identification by stool sample analysis.

Tapeworms, which are carried by fleas, are also identified by the ancient Egyptian technique of lifting a cat's tail and peering studiously at its anus. During this examination, the inspector is looking for small, white tapeworm segments that look like reborn stir-fried rice. A tapeworm can be eliminated only if the head of the tapeworm is killed by a deworming agent. Otherwise, the tapeworm will regenerate itself.

Trematodes are tiny flukes that live in the small intestines of their hosts. Cats generally become infested with trematodes after eating raw fish, frogs,

The life cycle of a tapeworm: The flea, which carries microscopic tapeworm larvae, bites a cat, transmitting the larvae to it. The larvae then migrate to the intestine, where they develop into a mature tapeworm composed of many flat segments. Each segment absorbs nutrients from the contents of the intestine.

or small rodents. Because few Birman owners allow their cats outdoors, there is little chance of Birmans becoming infected with trematodes unless a Birman hunts down an infected mouse indoors.

Worms, despite their repugnance, are not difficult to eliminate. If your cat needs to be dewormed, use a product prescribed by your veterinarian, and be sure to use it according to instructions.

Other varieties of internal parasites known as protozoa are usually one-celled organisms that may contain specialized structures for feeding and locomotion. After a cat ingests soil containing protozoan cysts, the cysts invade the lining of the bowel where they mature into adults and are shed in the feces. The protozoa coccidia that infect cats can be identified through stool sample analysis. Cats infected with coccidiosis must be isolated during treatment.

HOW-TO:
Caring for a Sick Cat

Cats appreciate and seek the regenerative power of solitude when they are sick. They expect you to appreciate and to respect that power as well. Thus, to nurse a sick cat is to strike a balance between respecting its desire for privacy and helping it to recover.

Most cats resist taking pills as though they were poison. Cats will also lick any "foreign" material from their coats, especially if it is medicated. They object to being force-fed, and because their instincts tell them they are vulnerable and, therefore, ought to hide when they are sick, they must often be caged in order to be accessible when it is time for the 2:00 A.M. medication. For these reasons, the seriously ill or injured cat is better left in the care of your veterinarian, but cats with lesser ailments should be treated at home.

Isolation and Cleanliness

The first principle of home nursing care is that sick or convalescing cats should be iso-lated from other cats. The second rule is that persons handling sick or convalescing cats should wash their hands thoroughly and, if necessary, change their clothes before handling other cats. In fact, anyone handling a sick cat would do well to wear rubber gloves. What is more, all bedding, food dishes, water bowls, and litter pans used by any cat suffering from a contagious disease should be disinfected with a nontoxic antiseptic. All leftover food, litter, soiled dressings, excrement, and other waste should be sealed in a plastic bag and placed immediately into an outdoor trash can.

The Confinement Cage

Sick cats are best confined to a double cage, 22 inches (56 cm) deep and tall and 44 inches (112 cm) wide in a warm, quiet, draft-free room. The cage should contain a litter pan, food dish, water bowl, and a cozy cat bed for the patient. Towels around three sides and over the top of the cage may also make the patient feel more secure. (Though a cat might not be up to playing, a toy spider hanging in one corner of the cage may eventually prove diverting.) If

the sick cat must be kept warm, put a cardboard box, with one side cut down for ease of entry and exit, in one corner of the cage; and put a heating pad covered with a towel in the bottom of the box. Leave a radio, set to an easy-listening or a nonhysterical talk station, playing softly. Groom the cat as usual if it will tolerate this. Otherwise, just hold and pet the cat gently. Do not spend too much time with it. Sleep is the second-best medicine in most cases.

Feeding a Sick Cat

Because many sick cats are not eager to eat, you will be challenged to concoct something that your cat will find palatable. Forget balanced diets for the moment. Feed a sick cat anything it will eat. Cats recovering from upper respiratory infections may not be able to smell most foods. Use strong-smelling food like sardines or tuna fish or meat that has been seasoned liberally with garlic. If a cat accepts any of these, you can balance the menu as time passes.

Sliced turkey breast from the deli is a great favorite of sick cats. So is baby food. Some cats will eat a molasseslike, high-calorie food substitute available from your veterinarian.

To make sure the patient does not become dehydrated, resort to any fluid you have to in order to get your cat to drink: water, beef broth, chicken broth, or evaporated milk mixed with baby cereal, egg yolk, Karo syrup, and a pinch of salt. If your cat is extremely weak, you may have to administer fluids

Sick cats appreciate and instinctively seek the regenerative powers of solitude.

with an eyedropper or a syringe. (see Supplemental Feeding, page 84).

Cats too sick to eat on their own will have to be fed with a syringe.

Pilling the Cat

Persuading most cats to accept a pill is always a tenuous proposition at best. Some people seem to have been born with a knack for pilling. They grasp the top of a cat's head in one hand, pinching the corners of its mouth with thumb and middle finger or ring finger to force the mouth open, drop the pill onto the back of the cat's tongue, jab an index finger quickly against the back of the cat's throat, withdraw the finger, hold the cat's mouth shut, then blow quickly into the cat's face to startle it and to make it swallow. Persons lacking this agility and self-confidence resort to pill guns, which still require that someone pry open a cat's mouth to insert the gun, or to hiding ground-up pills in butter, a lump of hamburger, or a mound of baby food.

Force-feeding

Force-feeding is less strenuous on your cat, and its initial resistance may subside when it realizes that the stuff you are insinuating into its mouth tastes good. The technique for force-feeding is similar to that for pilling: Hold the cat's head from the top. Place your thumb against one corner of the mouth and your middle finger or ring finger against the other corner. Squeeze the mouth open. Put a dollop of food on the index finger of your free hand and rub it onto the roof of the mouth. Relax the pressure on the sides of the face, allowing the mouth to close, but keep your cat restrained or else it might shake the food out. Putting a small dab of food on your cat's nose, from which the food will be promptly licked, is another way of getting your cat to take some nourishment.

If you are feeding liquid foods, put them into a syringe, open your cat's mouth as above, then squeeze some of the liquid into the pocket formed where the upper and lower lips meet. Administer the liquid slowly, allowing your cat time to swallow. Five cc syringes are easily manipulated. Buy a supply of them and change them frequently.

Skin Medicating

After applying any skin medication, hold your cat or play with it quietly for a few minutes to distract it so that it will not lick the medication off before it has had a chance to do any good. If skin medication must remain undisturbed for a longer period of time, ask your veterinarian to show you how to fashion an Elizabethan collar that will prevent your cat from licking itself.

When the business of pilling, force-feeding, or medicating your cat is finished, apologize for the intrusion and explain that you are really trying to help. Then sit with your Birman quietly for a while, commiserating.

This Birman kitten has already discovered the secret of life: It pays to look innocent.

The protozoan most familiar to cat owners is *Toxoplasma gondii*. This familiarity is occasioned by the fact that *T. gondii* can also infect humans (see Can Your Cat Make You Sick?, page 57).

Putting the Bite on Dental Problems

Kittens have 26 teeth; adult cats have 30. The adult cat's margin of dental victory is provided by its four molars, which kittens do not have. Molars are the teeth located nearest the throat. There are two upper molars, one on each side of the mouth, and two lower molars, similarly placed.

A kitten's teeth are known as deciduous teeth (from the Latin *deciduus*, meaning "tending to fall"). Smaller and more slender than adult teeth, kitten teeth begin to emerge when the kitten is 11 to 15 days old. The incisors are the first teeth to appear. They are the

12 tiny teeth—six upper and six lower—located in the front of the mouth.

The next kitten teeth to emerge are the four canine teeth, which are the large, fanglike models situated on either side of the upper and lower incisors. The canine teeth emerge between 17 and 19 days after a kitten is born.

The last kitten teeth to emerge are the ten premolars, located behind the upper and lower canines. The premolars make their appearance between 37 and 60 days after birth.

When kittens are three and a half to four months old, they begin to lose their baby teeth. Their permanent teeth should all be in place by the time kittens are six months of age.

At any age, a cat's teeth should be impeccably white and clean, and its breath, while it may not resemble peaches and cream, should not smell like freshly scattered fertilizer either. Moreover, the gums and tissues of a cat's mouth should be pink, but for the black pigment spots that some cats have on their gums. Firm-feeling, pink gums that adhere snugly to a cat's teeth are a sign of good health. Pale gums are a warning that a cat may be bleeding internally or suffering from anemia or any of a number of systemic diseases.

Gingivitis

Gingivitis, the presence of which is betrayed by a raw-looking, red line where the gums meet the teeth, is a frequent and stubborn problem in cats. Mild gingivitis may be tolerated by a cat without causing any ill effects. More serious gingivitis is accompanied by drooling and bad breath.

Gingivitis can result from an accumulation of plaque and tartar on a cat's teeth. When plaque spreads beneath the gums, it inflames them, causes redness and swelling, and eventual loosening of the teeth.

Gingivitis also can be caused by viruses such as feline calicivirus and feline leukemia virus.

Dental Care

Those owners blessed with patience and with tolerant cats can clean their cats' teeth by rubbing them with a soft cloth (a cotton swab, a clean finger, a child's toothbrush, or a gauze pad) that has been dipped into dilute hydrogen peroxide, bicarbonate of soda, or saltwater. Do not use human toothpaste on your cat. The foaming agent it contains can cause gastric problems. Avoid using baking soda or salt to clean your cat's teeth. These substances do not remove plaque effectively, and they contain sodium, which can be harmful to older cats with heart disease. Whether your cat allows you to "brush" its teeth daily, weekly, or when the moon is new, its teeth should be cleaned professionally at least once a year.

Can Your Cat Make You Sick?

People are the greatest source of infection to other people, but cats are also capable of giving their owners a dose of unpleasantness. The technical name for an animal disease that is communicable to humans is zoonosis. There are more than 200 known zoonoses, but only a few are associated with pets, and many of the pet-borne zoonoses are not passed on from one human to another.

Rabies

Rabies is a viral infection that cannot be treated with antibiotics, nor does it succumb to antibodies produced by our immune systems. Rabies is fatal for virtually all its unvaccinated victims.

The rabies virus is present in the saliva of infected animals. The disease is spread from a rabid animal to a new victim when saliva enters the victim's body through any of three routes: skin

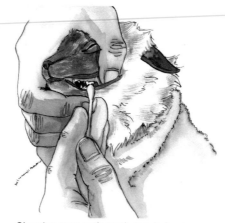

Cleaning your cat's teeth regularly can prevent dental problems from putting the bite on its health.

punctured by a bite from an infected carrier, already broken skin, or mucous membranes such as the tissues lining the nose or mouth. Because rabies is transmitted through infected saliva, not from a bite itself, a bite or a scratch from a rabid animal or any form of contact that might bring its saliva in touch with broken skin or mucous membranes constitutes exposure to rabies.

A Birman taking a solemn vow that it will not scratch the sofa.

For several days or even months following exposure, the rabies virus reproduces at the site where it entered the body. Eventually it travels through the central nervous system to the brain and produces signs of illness. Those signs take two forms, furious and dumb. A cat with furious (or mad dog) rabies will attack anything that moves. A cat with dumb (or paralytic) rabies suffers paralysis of the muscles that control swallowing, which may cause the cat to drool, suffer coughing spells, and paw at its mouth.

If you find your Birman playing with a bat or a mouse that has gained entrance to your house, kill the intruder and take it to your local health department laboratory. Whatever method you choose for killing the intruder, be sure not to damage its head too severely because accurate rabies testing is predicated on a supply of well-preserved brain tissue. It is important to take the dead animal in for testing. Be sure to wear gloves when handling the dead animal because tests can reveal within a few days whether or not the animal was rabid. Otherwise, you will have to quarantine your cat for several months to see whether it develops symptoms of rabies. Quarantine regulations, which vary from state to state, can be obtained from the department of public health.

Unless you live in Hawaii, which is rabies-free, or in an urban center that is animal-free, wildlife infected with rabies probably lives in your neighborhood. Raccoons, skunks, foxes, coyotes, and bats are all rabies-carrying species. Your chances of visits from such animals will be reduced if you do not leave food outside for any animals, and if you keep garbage receptacles secure against raids by roaming domestic animals and foraging wildlife.

Toxoplasmosis

Cats are the definitive host for *Toxoplasma gondii,* the protozoan parasite that causes toxoplasmosis (A definitive host is one in which the adult or sexually mature stage of the parasite is produced.). Cats can become infected by *T. gondii* after eating cysts present in the tissue of infected prey or other raw meat, by ingesting oocysts (eggs) picked up from contaminated soil upon which infected animals have defecated, or by eating tachyzoites, a form of *T. gondii* present in infected animals. Thus, outdoor cats or cats that come into contact with outdoor cats are most likely to become infected.

In other animals and humans, *T. gondii* moves immediately from the intestines to other body tissues. In cats it multiplies in the wall of the small intestine, producing oocysts, which are excreted (shed) in the feces for one or two weeks. About one to three days after being shed, the oocysts usually become infectious to animals and humans. Once a cat's immune system responds to *T. gondii,* the cat stops shedding oocysts. Although 30 to 80 percent of domestic cats have been infected by *T. gondii,* most cats do not develop clinical toxoplasmosis.

Cats most likely to become clinical are kittens, young adults, and adults whose immune systems have been weakened by the feline leukemia or feline immunodeficiency viruses. Because symptoms of toxoplasmosis—pneumonia, liver failure, seizures, and paralysis—mimic those of other diseases, making a definitive diagnosis is hard. In many cases, especially in young kittens, the disease runs its course swiftly and fatally.

The most common source of *T. gondii* infection in humans is raw or undercooked meat containing tissue cysts. Humans also can be infected after handling a cat that is shedding oocysts—or cleaning that cat's litter pan—and then inadvertently touching their mouths.

According to an Information Bulletin published by the Cornell Feline Health Center, 30 to 50 percent of the world's human population has been exposed to *T. gondii*. Persons infected by this parasite usually do not develop clinical toxoplasmosis, and most people are never aware they have been infected. Occasionally, *T. gondii* infection in humans leads to swollen glands, sometimes accompanied by fever, headache, and fatigue; but more serious infections usually develop only in persons with weakened immune systems.

T. gondii poses the greatest risk to the fetuses of women who are infected for the first time during pregnancy, particularly during the first trimester of pregnancy. Fortunately, if a woman previously infected by *T. gondii* is re-exposed to the parasite during pregnancy, her immune system, which now contains toxoplasmosis antibodies, will destroy the parasite before it reaches her fetus.

The other group with high susceptibility to infection by *T. gondii* includes people with compromised immune systems. This latter group consists of AIDS patients and transplant recipients taking drugs that prevent organ rejection by suppressing the immune system.

The Centers for Disease Control report that *T. gondii* is responsible for roughly 3,000 human congenital infections every year—about one third to one half of the babies born to mothers who have been exposed to *T. gondii* during pregnancy. Most women infected during pregnancy exhibit no signs of the infection, but when *T. gondii* crosses the placenta and infects the fetus, the fetus may die or develop into a visually and/or mentally impaired child. Symptoms may be present at birth, or may take weeks, months, or even years to appear.

Although most adults who develop toxoplasmosis usually recover, the parasites never leave their hosts entirely. When the immune system fails, the parasites are free to run amuck, and fre-quently do. Thus, people with AIDS are in double jeopardy—from reinfection or future infection. Transplant patients, in addition to being subject to the same perils, can contract the disease after acquiring *T. gondii* from a donor organ.

To minimize the risk of infection by *T. gondii*: Cook meat to an internal temperature of 158°F (70°C) for at least 15 to 30 minutes. Clean thoroughly any kitchen counter tops or utensils with which meat has come into contact. Avoid unpasteurized dairy products. Wash all vegetables before cooking them. Do not allow cats on the kitchen table. Remove solid waste from litter pans at least every 24 hours in order to remove oocysts before they become infective. Do not feed raw meat to cats. Do not allow your cat outdoors. Disinfect litter pans with scalding water. Wear rubber gloves while gardening. Cover children's sandboxes. If you are pregnant, have AIDS, or are taking immune system-suppressing drugs, have someone clean the litter pan for you. Otherwise, wear rubber gloves when you do and wash your hands vigorously afterwards.

Cats and humans can be tested for antibodies to *T. gondii*. In healthy cats, the presence of antibodies in the blood indicates that an animal has been exposed to the parasite in the past, has mounted a defense against the invasion, is most probably immune to further infection, and is not shedding oocysts. (There is a potential for antibody-positive cats to shed upon reinfection, but that potential is slight.) A healthy, antibody-negative cat is susceptible to infection upon exposure to *T. gondii*.

In healthy humans, the presence of antibodies means that a fetus is not at risk should a woman become re-exposed to *T. gondii* during pregnancy. An antibody-negative woman is at risk of transmitting *T. gondii* to her fetus if she becomes infected during pregnancy.

Cat Scratch Fever

This disease, one of the few to be noted in a popular song, visits people who are scratched, bitten, or licked by a cat carrying the bacteria that causes cat scratch fever. The first indication of the disease in humans is the appearance of a small skin nodule at the site of contact or inoculation. Additional symptoms include fatigue, loss of appetite, headaches, and enlargement of the lymph nodes near the site of infection, e.g., the armpit if you are scratched on the arm, the groin if you are scratched on the leg. Occasionally, cat scratch fever also produces severe skin rashes, bone lesions, and seizures.

Kittens or newly acquired cats are most likely to transmit cat scratch fever to humans. The interval between the time a person is infected by a cat and the time that lesions appear varies from three to 14 days. Fortunately, cat

The Birman's semilong coat does not require as much maintenance as the coats of some longhair breeds.

scratch fever is usually a benign, self-limiting disease that does not require treatment. If you are bitten by your Birman, a most unlikely event, be sure to clean the wound thoroughly; and if you begin to feel tired or feverish shortly after being bitten, be sure to see your physician. Cat scratch fever is treatable with antibiotics such as gentamycin.

Worms

People can also be infected by some of the worms their cats carry. In cases of *cutaneous larva migrans*, the larvae of several species of hookworms penetrate the skin after people have come into contact with soil that harbors these larvae. The larvae produce small bumps where they enter the body, and as the larvae migrate through the skin, they leave behind tunnels over which blisters form. The tissues react to this migration by itching, mightily, and the resulting scratching that most people do is responsible for the secondary bacterial infection.

Hookworm larvae can stay under the skin for several months. Eventually, the symptoms they cause disappear spontaneously, but their disappearance can be hastened if people are treated with an anthelmintic (deworming agent).

Roundworm eggs living in soil where cats have defecated are sometimes ingested by humans, primarily children. The eggs may be rejected by the body. If not, they hatch in the intestine and migrate to various parts of the body. The disease that roundworms produce is called *visceral larva migrans*. Its symptoms—inflammation of the lungs, swollen liver, abdominal pain, muscle and joint aches, cough, rashes, skin nodules, visual defects, and convulsions—depend on the location of the sites to which the roundworms migrate. *Visceral larva migrans* runs its course in about a year.

Understanding Your Birman

Although cats are commonly believed to be enigmatic, we are no less able to know the contents of their minds than we are to know the thoughts of any other beings—human or nonhuman. A great measure of the cat's celebrated reserve is a comparative phenomenon arising from the fact that cats are much less inclined than are dogs to tell you what they are thinking and, especially, feeling. Moreover, when a cat does talk, its language is more subtle and self-contained than a dog's tail-wagging, rump-shaking, tongue-lolling, effervescent dialect.

All Things Considered

Cats are misunderstood and misrepresented more than any other domesticated animal. No creature has had more unfortunate press than has the cat, and that bad press has been exceeded only by the cat's extreme reversals of fortune. Deified during the Egyptian empire, vilified in the High Middle Ages, the cat has also been romanticized by everyone from Lewis Carroll to Ernest Hemingway. Despite all that has been said about and against them, cats are neither demon nor deity, and they are certainly not the haughty curmudgeons that some cartoonists and a few retrograde feature writers would have us believe.

Cats, as a race, are not uncommonly sly, mysterious, arrogant, remote, ethereal, intimidating, or all that terribly complex. Nor were they created so that humans might caress the tiger. A cat is nobody's stand-in. And for all their quiet sovereignty, not to mention their guiding inclination to do what they wish and to get what they want, cats are quite willing to dance attendance on our comings and goings as if they were front-page news. The cats' dance, however, is a minuet, not a polka. Their song a chanson, not an anthem. Their poetry a lyric, not an epic. They are, nonetheless, capable of playing the clown, but they are quick to repair any pulls in their dignity.

The cat is not to blame because its thoughts are seldom projected beyond the backs of its eyes while the dog's face is as full of emotion as a drive-in movie screen. Lloyd Alexander, the author of award-winning children's

Two Birmans engaged in pillow talk.

books and *My Five Tigers,* the best book of true cat stories—indeed, of any cat stories—anywhere, asks if "perhaps a small part of the cat's notorious reserve and aloofness is something like whistling in the dark." What is most remarkable about this observation is that Alexander made it nearly four decades ago, long before cats had become ubiquitous fixtures on greeting cards and coffee mugs. "A cat's life can be as difficult as our own," said Alexander, "and it may be that we comfort them for being cats as much as they comfort us for being human."

Domestication and Feline Behavior

The transcendent clue to understanding the cat, of which the Birman is a loving, gentle specimen, is contained in the circumstances of the cat's domestication. Although they were contemporaries of prehistoric people in many places, cats were among the last animals to be domesticated. Our ancestors had gentled at least a dozen other animals—beginning with dogs, reindeer, goats, and sheep, more than 10,000 years ago—before developing a relationship with cats.

Most observers agree that cats were first domesticated in Egypt, where, many people also believe, they had been introduced originally by Ethiopians. The earliest known Egyptian pictorial representations of cats appeared in the third millennium B.C. Though researchers are not unanimous in the belief that these cats were domesticated, virtually everyone who has studied the matter concedes that cats were fully domesticated in Egypt by 1600 B.C.

Further disagreement attends the discussion of the manner in which cats were domesticated. However it came to pass, cats were domesticated roughly 5,000 years ago as an agrarian society evolved in Egypt and wild cats moved closer to towns and villages, attracted by discarded food and the large populations of rats and mice that thrived in granaries. When cats demonstrated their skill at policing stores of grain, farmers began feeding them to entice them to remain on the job.

All animals domesticated before the cat had lived in some kind of communal arrangement on which their biological and social well-being depended. Consequently, they all exhibited certain predictors of domestication. Chief among them were membership in a large social group, acceptance of a hierarchical group structure, and a promiscuous lifestyle. But with the exception of promiscuity, the cat did not score high on these or most other variables that correlate with subsequent domestic status.

The ability to function in a tightly structured group contributes more than any other attribute to ease of domestication and to an animal's attachment to the domesticating species. This ability further explains, by its absence, why the cat does not regard humans with the same incessant affection as the dog, or the same patient stoicism as the horse. These species follow the lead of the dominant member of the pack or herd, usually the alpha female. In an equine herd, for example, when the alpha mare stops to graze, the herd stops, too. When the mare takes off at a gallop, the herd follows. When the mare decides to rest, the herd settles down as well.

This centuries-old, follow-the-leader instinct disposes Trigger and Lassie to accept humans as the top dogs in their lives, but no such instinct prevails upon Garfield, who kept his own hours and his own counsel for thousands of centuries before signing a series of one-generation-only contracts to do mouse work for humans. Therefore, whereas the dog is prewired to seek the goodwill of the alpha human and to show that human unbounded loyalty and affection, the cat is inclined to offer its friendship to those who deserve it and to keep its emotions to itself.

What is more, the interval since the cat was first domesticated is but a blink in time's steady gaze; and as one zoologist has remarked, cats are "an instructive example of a species which is only in the first stage of domestication, perfectly capable of still becoming feral, and comparatively little altered" vis-à-vis its distant ancestors. One could even argue that pedigreed cats are the only truly domesticated felines because they are the only cats from whom we have usurped reproductive choices—an important element of the domestication process.

People have been arranging unions between pedigreed cats for little more than 120 years, and most of those unions were contrived on the basis of conformation, not temperament. Nonetheless, there are already significant behavioral differences between domestic and pedigreed cats. The latter, by and large, are more dependent on and more closely bonded to humans than are a great many domesticated and virtually all feral cats.

Perhaps in time the pedigreed cat will evolve into a companion entirely more fawning than formal. Cats are known for their ability to exploit the most precarious of niches. If people want cats to fetch the newspaper, and set about breeding cats selectively with that end in mind, the late twenty-first-century feline no doubt will be described by writers as categorically different from the cat of the late twentieth century. Who is to say, in fact, that the capacity for a more involved relationship with humans has not been part of the cat's repertoire all along? A talent the cat has been waiting for us to discover.

The Rites of Communal Living

In the back alleys of our cities, the backyards of suburbia, and the backwoods and countryside of rural America, feral cats lead mostly first-person-singular lives. Low population densities, well-established rituals, clearly defined territories, limited and rather circumscribed interactions between adult cats, and one-tom-per-commonwealth living arrangements characterize the feral cat's existence.

Cats that live indoors, particularly in multicat confederations are asked—in exchange for regular meals and climate-controlled lodging—to abide conditions that violate the natural order. In one British study of cat-population densities, researchers found that feral cats in East London, where cats live in the most crowded conditions, had two-hundredths of an acre, or 871 square feet (81 sq m) to call their own. Yet few households and fewer catteries are large enough to provide this minimal acreage for every cat in residence. Obviously, indoor cats must live in smaller "territories" than do outdoor cats and, in multicat households, must tolerate greater interaction with other adult cats. These departures from a cat's natural lifestyle can lead to deviations in natural behavior and to greater susceptibility to stress and disease. The logistics of communal living may cause some cats to try to dominate others in the course of establishing a pecking order with regard to who eats before whom and who sleeps in what window. Crowded living arrangements may cause some cats to ignore their litter pans periodically and may result in the rapid spread of parasites or illness if one member of the community becomes infected.

How Birmans Communicate

Communication with your Birman includes the exchange of thoughts, feelings, needs, moods, information, trust, and desires. Communication involves listening as well as speaking. When conversing with your Birman, you should listen not only with your ears but with your eyes. You should speak not only with your voice but with gestures, too.

You should also speak quietly. Birmans are wont to save their voices for certain occasions, and on those occasions the Birman voice is usually soft. No matter what the circumstance, when your Birman speaks to you, there is a reason. Birmans are not the type to speak merely to admire the sound of their own voices. You should, therefore, always respond when your Birman speaks. If Ruffles is shut in the closet, she wants to hear how sorry you are for her misfortune and how you will never let this indignity happen again. If her fur has been tousled while you were grooming her, she wants a similar apology. When she wakes you up for breakfast, she would like a cheery "good morning" and some food on her plate.

Cats speak volumes with their bodies. Upper left: a friendly approach. Upper right: wariness. Lower left: bristling hostility. Lower right: fearful submission.

The Birman's most endearing verbal communication is the silent meow. This "vocalization" is not peculiar to Birmans, but it is no less captivating for being universal. A silent meow is just that—a cat opens its mouth and mimes the word meow, but no sound emerges. Silent meows function as greetings, terms of endearment, all-purpose, unspecified complaints, and as the feline equivalents of baying at the moon.

Birmans are more likely to communicate with their bodies than with their voices. From the tips of their noses to the ends of their tails, they are like electronic bulletin boards on which a continuous series of messages flows.

Cats can generate at least three of those messages with their tails. Carried erect at a 90-degree angle to the body, the tail broadcasts a message of good cheer and camaraderie. Carried at a less jaunty angle and puffed out in bristling display, the tail is a declaration of war. Twitching slowly from side to side, the tail signals annoyance. The faster the twitch, the greater the itch, and if twitch turns to lash, beware—fireworks are about to ensue.

A Birman uses its hindquarters to declare affection and trust. This form of communication, in which a cat brushes past the object of its affection and then positions its hindquarters in firsthand proximity to the object's face, may take the cat-owning novice by surprise, especially if cat and novice are enjoying a nap together. Indeed, most long-time cat owners would prefer that their cats said it with flowers instead.

A more conventional expression of fondness is the full-body flop, a maneuver in which a cat lands first on its side, then rolls onto its back, finally ending up in a semicircle. This fetching invitation to a belly rub usually is inspired by a cat's exuberance at being stroked along its spine or scratched at the base of its tail. Be cautious in accepting this invitation, however, because many cats are ticklish on their bellies. When you reach past their upturned paws to scratch their bellies, you are putting your arm at some risk. Should the cat take it into its head to grasp your arm between its front paws and to rabbit kick with its back paws, your arm could be in for a shredding. Do not panic and try to withdraw your arm suddenly. That will make your situation more perilous because you will be pulling your tender skin against your cat's talonlike claws. Instead of moving your arm backward toward you, move it forward and down through the cat's front legs. Because that is the direction in which your upside-down cat's claws are pointed, you will be disengaging your flesh from their grasp.

From head to tail this Birman communicates an inquisitive air.

Right side up, the Birman taps out a variety of messages with its paws. A paw raised softly to a person's cheek or laid gently on the arm is a sign of attachment. A series of taps on the leg or arm is an attempt to bring the human to attention. A smart whack with the claws sheathed is a warning that you have violated a cat's sense of propriety. Such warnings often are issued while a cat that is being groomed is touched in a spot that is sensitive or ticklish.

Like its tail, a Birman's ears convey different messages and emotions. Birmans swivel their ears in response to new sounds in the vicinity. They flatten their ears and extend them to the side in response to a frightening stimulus, and they curl their ears backward in anger.

Cats greet their two-legged and four-legged friends in well-defined ceremonies. A cat, its tail erect in greeting, will approach a friend and then rub its cheek against the cheek, neck, or face of that friend. This rite not only indi-

cates cordiality; it is a request for permission to enter another individual's air space, and it leaves a trace of the approaching cat's scent on its friend.

If looks could kill, somebody should start writing the photographer's obituary.

Communicating with Your Birman

Cats are more comfortable when we are communicating with them on their level than when we approach them from a superior position. Cats are apt to associate creatures that loom large with predators. Therefore, when you are greeting your Birman, you should crouch down and extend your slightly curled hand, knuckles facing away from you, toward the cat, allowing it a chance to sniff and to rub up against your hand if the cat wishes.

In all your interactions with your cat, try to mimic its sense of order, civility, and decorum. Do not make any abrupt movements or any sudden, loud noises. Do not lift the cat up if it does not enjoy being carried, and by all means do not stare long and lovingly into its eyes. Cats regard staring as an insult.

Aside from communicating your joy in its presence, which you should do with hugs, pets, and kisses as well as words, the other message you will want to convey to your cat is your displeasure at something it has just done or is about to do.

The best way to teach your cat to refrain from doing something you do not want it doing is to establish an association between the proscribed conduct and an unpleasant occurrence. Suppose you are sitting at the kitchen table and your kitten races across the floor and begins climbing your leg, which kittens are likely to do. If its claws sink deep enough into your leg, you might scream in pain, and this might be enough to send your kitten on its way—for now. But even if the pain is not severe this time, reach down quickly, remove the kitten from your leg, set it on the floor facing away from you, and bark no. If your kitten assaults your leg again, even if not until the following day, remove the kitten, bark no, and clap your hands sharply for emphasis. Better yet, if you notice your pet eyeing your leg with bad intent, say no before kitty gets a chance to leap.

The youngest feline capable of scaling a human leg eventually will connect your sharp voice and other unpleasant noises with unwanted behavior. But even the wisest cat has a limited retention span, about 20 seconds, to be precise. Thus, you are wasting your time and your cat's goodwill by taking it to the scene of a crime, such as a broken knickknack or a soiled spot on the carpet, and reprimanding it sharply for something that happened hours or minutes ago. The only lesson your cat will learn from this delayed reprimand is that humans sometimes act peculiarly for no good reason.

Cat Shows

If weekends are no longer the carefree revels they used to be, if the wind has gone out of the yard sales, if flea markets have lost their bite, if you are weary of all those dowdy television chefs who mince, dice, slice, and sauté the weekend long, if you are adrift from Friday until Monday because all the interesting support groups meet during the week, then may we suggest a splendid and satisfying diversion—the cat show. A cat show celebrates the bond that exists between people and their cats, and there is much to see and to experience at this celebration: Majestic cats in dazzling display, vendors who offer the finest in feline accessories, boutiques that overflow with people gifts for you or your cat-loving friends, and food concessions in case you work up an appetite carrying around all the things you have bought.

Development of the Cat Fancy

Once humankind had begun domesticating animals, there was bound to be some fraternizing between the species, for the appeal of animals is such that only the most hardhearted people can view them in a completely utilitarian, livestock manner. As soon as there is fraternizing between the species, the attitudes of humans toward their animals undergo powerful transformations. To be sure, humans have been singing a variation of the my-dog's-bigger-than-your-dog theme for thousands of years. One of those variations is the cat fancy.

The first known cat show was held at the St. Giles Fair in England in 1598, the year Shakespeare published *Much Ado About Nothing.* We do not know how many cats were entered in the St. Giles show, who the judges were, or by what criteria the cats were evaluated. We can assume that cat shows were an idea whose time had not yet come, for 273 years passed before the next recorded cat show took place. That one, which was the face-off that launched the modern-day cat fancy, was held in 1871 in London's Crystal Palace. Harrison Weir, who organized this event and served on the panel of judges, also wrote the standards by which different breeds and varieties of cats entered in the show were appraised. In 1887, Weir was elected president of the newly formed National Cat Club (NCC) in England. The NCC established a stud book and register, and thus began the custom of keeping track of cats' ancestors.

An illustrator's rendering of the first cat show, held in 1598 at the St. Giles Fair in England, long before the invention of spandex.

The birth of the cat fancy in the United States occurred officially on May 8, 1895, when an Englishman named James T. Hyde organized a cat show in Madison Square Garden in New York. One hundred and twenty-five exhibitors—and 176 cats—were at this coming out party in the garden, where temperatures reached 96°F (36°C). The following year, the American Cat Club was formed for the purposes of maintaining a stud book, verifying pedigrees, sponsoring shows, and promoting the welfare of cats. Today, there are seven different cat associations in North America (see Useful Addresses and Literature, page 93). They register about 80,000 cats and license 850 shows each year. The cat associations also publish breed standards and show rules; charter clubs; train, examine, and license judges; enforce by-laws and show rules; award titles to cats that have earned them in the show ring; approve breed standards; recognize new breeds and colors; and present national and/or regional awards annually to the highest-scoring cats and kittens shown during the preceding year. In addition, several of the larger associations publish newsletters, magazines, and yearbooks.

A Birman imitating art.

Where the Shows Are

Cat magazines list hundreds of shows held each year in the United States and Canada. If these magazines are not available at the newsstand, call one of their subscription departments (see Useful Addresses and Literature, page 93) and ask to buy the latest issue. Newspapers, too, may contain notices for cat shows in the "Pets" section of the classified ads or in the notices of coming events in the "Living," "Lifestyle," or "Weekend" sections. The various cat-registering bodies in North America that license shows (see page 93) may also be helpful in this regard. Call one of them and ask for a list of the clubs and/or shows in your area.

Once you have obtained information about a show, call the club presenting the show to find out how many vendors will be on hand, how many cats will be competing, how much you will have to pay to attend the show, the hours during which the show will be held, and how to get to the show hall if necessary. Some shows have only a few vendors selling basic cat care products; other shows are veritable shopping malls.

Should You Show Your Cat?

A cat show does not have to be a spectator affair. If you bought a show-quality Birman, you will more than likely want to show it; and even if you bought a pet-quality cat that you had no intention of showing, you might change your mind once you have witnessed the household-pet competition at a show. Whatever the case and whenever the show bug lands on your morning newspaper, do not enter your cat in a show until you have attended a few shows yourself to observe prevailing customs and to appraise the competition. If you decide to have a go at showing, the following information will help to make that experience as stress-free as possible. No show, of course, is ever completely stress-free. If it is, you either are not taking it seriously enough or you have been showing too long.

The Show Flyer and Entry Form

Show advertisements in cat magazines usually contain the name, address, and phone number of the entry clerk for that event. If you are interested in entering your cat in a show, write or phone the entry clerk to request a show flyer and an entry form.

The flyer provides the show hall location, the time the show begins, and the hours when exhibitors can check in their cats. The flyer also discloses whether the show committee will provide litter, litter pans, and cat food for all entries, and what special trophies or prizes will be awarded at the show. Flyers announce the entry fee, the date on which the club will stop taking entries, and the judges who will officiate at the show. Flyers remind exhibitors that all household pet entries must be neutered or spayed, that all cats' inoculations should be up to date, that cats from catteries where infectious illness has occurred during the last 21 days are not allowed in the show hall, and, if local law requires, that exhibitors must bring along proof that their cats have been vaccinated against rabies.

Filling out the entry form, while not as taxing as filling out the 1040 long form and several of its attendant schedules, still requires some attention to details. On the entry form an exhibitor provides the name of the cat being shown, its owner's name, the cat's breed, color, registration number, date of birth, parents, sex, and eye color, the class in which the cat will compete, the name of the person, if any, who will exhibit the cat for its owner, and the name of the person,

Kittens are self-starting groomers. They start grooming themselves at an early age.

if any, with whom an exhibitor would like to be benched. (Each cat entered in a show is "benched" or assigned to a cage where it remains when it is not being judged.) If an exhibitor has any questions about completing an entry form, entry clerks will answer them cheerfully before nine or ten o'clock at night.

Once an entry form is completed, the exhibitor mails it with the appropriate fee to the entry clerk. Two-day

Paperwork in hand, a Birman owner is ready for show time.

shows cost $30 to $60, depending on the number of times a cat will be judged. One-day shows are proportionately less expensive.

The number of entries at a show usually is limited, and shows often reach their quota before the advertised closing date. To avoid being shut out, exhibitors should mail their entry forms at least two or three weeks prior to that date. If you enter a show and do not receive confirmation within two weeks after mailing your entry, phone the entry clerk to ask if the entry has been received.

Among the details in the entry confirmation are directions to the show hall, a list of motels near the hall, and a facsimile of the exhibitor's cat's listing in the show catalog. Exhibitors should proofread the confirmation to be sure all names are spelled correctly, the cat's registration number is accurate, and the cat has been entered in the correct class. Errors should be reported immediately to the entry clerk. After checking the confirmation, exhibitors should keep it in a safe, easy-to-recall place.

Provisions for a Show

During a show, cats remain in their assigned benching cages when not being judged. Exhibitors are expected to bring curtains for the sides and back of the benching cage and a rug or a towel for the cage floor. Most show cages are small: 22 inches (56 cm) long, wide, and tall. For an extra $10 to $20, exhibitors can order a double cage when they send in their entry blanks. A double cage provides more room in which a cat can stretch its legs, and the extra chair that comes with a double cage provides a convenient footrest for an exhibitor. Most double cages are 22 inches (56 cm) deep and tall and 44 inches (112 cm) wide.

Cage decorations vary with an exhibitor's taste, budget, sewing ability, and sense of style. Some exhibitors dress up their cages with lavish, hand-sewn curtains and precious little four-poster beds. Other exhibitors prefer a Quaker-plain look with bath towels held in place by metal clamps. A few exhibitors bring their own cages, which often resemble a cross between a habitrail for cats and a miniature intensive care unit. Personal aesthetics notwithstanding, minimum show requirements decree that cage curtains be fastened securely inside the cage and that they cover both the sides and the back of the cage. Many exhibitors also cover the tops of their cages, creating a more cozy environment for their cats.

Like fashions in cage curtains, the number of incidental items packed for a show is determined by personal comfort. Some exhibitors trundle into a show hall with enough provisions for a two-month stay in a biosphere. Others pack more temperately. The list on page 71 is offered to assist the novice exhibitor in planning his or her trousseau.

Nonammonia-based disinfectant is necessary for wiping down the benching cage and any suspicious surfaces in the hotel room. Pipe cleaners are handy for securing any loose corners of the cage. A small, TV-dinner-size table is useful for grooming. A bath towel makes a good cover for the table. A cardboard litter pan takes the worry out of being far from home. Show committees always provide litter, and they usually provide litter pans, but the seasoned exhibitor always carries a small, disposable, cardboard litter pan just in case.

Cats should be transported to shows in sturdy, heavy-molded-plastic carriers. These are available at pet shops, some airline cargo offices, and cat shows. The cat's journey will be more comfortable, especially if the ride is long or the cat is young, if the owner tapes a small litter pan to the floor inside the carrier. A disposable cardboard litter pan, cut in half and taped back together to create a smaller, square pan fits easily into a carrier. The rest of the carrier floor should be covered with a towel or disposable diaper.

Many exhibitors cover the outside of their carriers with fitted, quilted bonnets in cold weather. These bonnets, which resemble toaster covers, are available at shows or from companies that advertise in cat magazines. Exhibitors also can sew their own if they are "sew" inclined.

Show Hall Decorum

New exhibitors should check in early at the show hall. After obtaining their cats' cage numbers and a show catalog, the first orders of business are setting up the benching cage and finding out where the litter and the litter pans are stored. Many exhibitors spray the cage and cage floor (or bottom) with disinfectant and wipe it off carefully before decorating the cage and placing their cats in it. Cages are light enough to lift off their bottoms, which are supported by trestles about 3 feet (91 cm) high.

While the cage is on the floor, exhibitors can fit a rug or towel easily over the cage bottom. After setting the cage back on its trestle-supported bottom, lift up the top of the cage and install the cage curtains on the inside of the cage. Fill a litter pan with an inch (30 cm) of litter, and place the pan at one end of the cage. Make sure the cage top is fastened securely in case something in this foreign environment frightens your cat. Finally, put your cat into the cage with a favorite toy or two.

Because all show cages are double cages with a hinged, moveable divider in the center, exhibitors who get a single cage will be sharing a duplex with someone else. If that person has already set up his or her half of the cage, be careful not to disturb your

Basic Show Supplies

regular comb(s)	flea comb
cotton swabs	cotton balls
paper towels	facial tissues
washcloth(s)	bath towel(s)
scissors	eyedrops
cage curtains	cage rug
spray disinfectant	pen
pipe cleaners	can opener
bottle opener	cat toys
masking tape	adhesive tape
cellophane tape	first aid kit
cattery cards	cat food
water bowl	litter scoop
small metal clamps	safety pins
cardboard litter pan(s)	spoon
entry confirmation	cat shampoo
a small, TV-dinner-size table	
magazine, book, or small TV	
biodegradable paper plates	
snacks and hors d'oeuvres	
bottled water from home	
small plastic bag	
brushes and grooming powder if applicable	

neighbor's cage or cat when you are spraying and decorating your half of the cage.

Some exhibitors feed their cats after the cats have finished sniffing about their cages. Other exhibitors, who fed their cats before leaving for the show hall, wait until later in the day to feed. In either case, cats should be offered water when they are settled in their cages. Some exhibitors leave a water bowl in the cage all day. Others offer their cats a drink periodically throughout the day. If cats do not eat or drink in the show hall, exhibitors should offer them food and water as soon as they get home or to the hotel room.

How Cats Are Judged

A cat show actually comprises a number of individual shows held separately but concurrently in several judging rings throughout the show hall. With

"Winsome," adj., sweetly or innocently charming; winning; engaging (see also, "Birman").

few exceptions, every cat in the hall is eligible to compete in every individual show. Each show is presided over by a different judge who presents awards independent of the decisions of other judges. Therefore, a cat chosen best in show by the judge in Ring 1 may not receive the same award—or any award at all—from the judge in Ring 2.

Individual shows and their judges are classified as either all-breed or specialty. In an all-breed show, all cats entered compete for awards. In a specialty show, only those cats of similar coat length, or conformation and type, depending on the association, compete against each other.

Whether an individual show is all-breed, longhair specialty, or shorthair specialty, competition is held in five categories:

- Championship
- Altered
- Kitten
- New Breed or Color (sometimes called Provisional)
- Household pet

Championship competition is for unaltered, pedigreed cats that are at least eight months old. Altered competition is for neutered or spayed pedigreed cats that are at least eight months of age. Kitten competition is for pedigreed youngsters between the ages of four and eight months. New breed or color competition is for those breeds or colors that have not gained championship status. Household pet competition includes all nonpedigreed cats, and pet-quality pedigreed cats as well. Whatever their particulars, household pets that are older than eight months must be altered before they can be shown.

The judging schedule is printed in the show catalog or on a separate sheet provided with the catalog. Exhibitors should circle the rings in which their cats are scheduled to be judged. Exhibitors also should check to make sure their cats' names and attendant biographical data are printed correctly in the catalog. If there are any mistakes in this information, the exhibitor should tell the master clerk immediately.

Cats are called to the judging rings via the public address system. When the first Birman numbers are called, begin listening carefully for your cat's number.

Be sure to have a secure grip on your cat while carrying it to the judging ring. Hold your forearm slightly extended, palm up, parallel to the ground. Position your cat so that it straddles your forearm. Cup the cat's chest in your palm, securing one front leg between your thumb and forefinger, and the other front leg between your ring and little fingers. Should your cat become startled, stop for a moment, bring your forearm close to your body, and use your free hand to comfort your cat.

Upon arriving at the judging ring, find the cage with your cat's number on top and place your cat in that cage. Fasten the cage door securely, then take a seat in the gallery.

Like most eagerly awaited events in life, a cat's interval on the judging table is brief and somewhat anticlimactic, about 90 seconds on average. During that time, judges compare a cat to the standard for its breed. After handling all the entries in a class or division, judges hang ribbons whose text and colors proclaim the placement of each contestant that has merited a ribbon in the group. Then the clerk will dismiss the class by saying, "These cats can go back," or simply by turning down the numbers on the tops of cats' cages.

After a judge has examined all the cats competing in a category—all kittens, for example—it is time for finals,

A Birman conveying the impression that it won a glass bowl for being supremely attractive.

Show cats are evaluated according to a judge's subjective interpretation of an allegedly objective standard.

the encore in which the judge presents the top ten contestants in that category. During finals, the judge introduces the cats, usually in ascending order of merit, until the best cat (or kitten or alter, as the case may be) has been held aloft in triumph.

Adult cats compete for titles that vary somewhat in nomenclature and requirements from one association to the next. New exhibitors can learn the requirements of those associations in which they plan to have their cats compete by obtaining a copy of the association's show rules (see Useful Addresses and Literature, page 93) or by talking to a veteran exhibitor.

All associations offer champion and grand champion titles, and most award other titles beyond those. Champion, the lowest-ranking title, can be won in most associations even if a cat is the only entry in its class. Titles beyond champion are earned by defeating specified numbers of other cats, including other champions, in competition.

Mark Twain, who knew something about human nature and cats, once observed that it is difference of opinion that makes horse races. The same applies to cat shows. Judges spend one to two minutes evaluating each cat. They often make more than 200 of these rapid-fire assessments per show. For this display of expertise and subjectivity, judges receive from 35 cents to a dollar for every cat they judge. (Exhibitors who disagree with judges' decisions sometimes complain that a judge's opinion is not even worth that.)

Whatever the outcome, exhibitors would do well to remember that when they enter a cat in a show, they are paying to learn what several judges of varying degrees of competence and experience think about the exhibitor's cat at a brief moment in time. Those exhibitors who keep this in mind and who remember that, win or lose, their cats still will need to be fed tomorrow, will find that a cat show is a diverting way to spend a weekend.

Raising the Ultimate Birman

Anyone who gives a thought to breeding a litter of kittens for economic reasons should understand that few people profit as much from raising kittens properly as they would from working the same number of hours at minimum wage. Anyone who fancies breeding as a way to achieve fame in the show ring should understand that competition in the show ring is intense, and few breeders become overnight sensations. The laws of genetics are as fickle as they are immutable. Thus, few, if any, litters are filled with nothing but show-quality kittens. Anyone who wants to breed "just one litter so that the kids can witness the miracle of birth" should take the children to an animal shelter instead to let them observe the reality of unwanted animals and euthanasia.

Should You Breed Your Cat?

If you have not begun to suspect that the answer to this question is "most likely not," consider the following: With millions of healthy, nonpedigreed cats being destroyed annually for want of good homes, and with tens of thousands of purebred cats winding up in shelters each year, the decision to bring more kittens into the world should not be made frivolously. Indeed, most people should not make—or even consider making—this decision at all. Everyone who produces kittens contributes, albeit indirectly or marginally, to the surplus-cat population because pedigreed kittens are frequently purchased by people who might have adopted a homeless kitten from a shelter.

The Female's Heat Cycle

A heat cycle or season, more formally known as estrus, is a period of sexual advertisement and receptivity that occurs in most mammalian females, cats included. Estrus first occurs in the majority of female cats when they are between 7 and 12 months of age. (Male cats, which may be said to always be in season, generally become sexually mature and consumingly inquisitive between 9 and 12 months of age.)

Behind every cat in a shelter is a human who did not live up to his or her responsibilities.

Whispering sweet nothings.

Estrus in most cats is promoted by an increase in available light. Thus, after being sexually inactive throughout the fall of the year, cats begin to come into season in celebration of the new year and the increase in the length of the days. The main exceptions to this arrangement are those cats provided only with artificial light for 12 to 14 hours a day in a windowless, indoor environment. They will come into season every few weeks or so the year round. If cats are not bred during estrus, they normally go out of season after 6 to 9 days.

Ear to the ground, tail to the sky, a Birman in the throes of passion.

The interludes of peace and quiet between periods of estrus are called metestrus. They last, on average, between 9 and 13 days, but they may be as few as three or as many as 30 days long, depending on the cat owner's ill or good fortune.

Female cats repeat this in-a-while-out-a-while roundelay from January until March. Then, for reasons yet unknown, many females stop cycling temporarily. By June, most unbred females resume cycling and continue to do so until mid-September. If they are not with kittens by then, they remain out of season for about three months. This extended fallow period, called anestrus, may vary among breeds. In one study reported in the *Journal of Small Animal Practice* in 1977, 90 percent of the longhaired cats observed went into seasonal anestrus, but only 40 percent of the shorthaired cats did.

The Games Hormones Play

By the time the female begins rolling and calling, small, saclike follicles containing eggs have formed on her ovaries. An average of two to four follicles swell up and emerge on the surface of each ovary. After 10 to 15 days the follicles—round, pink, and slightly raised on the ovarian surface—approach maturity.

Soon after the follicles begin development, the ovaries secrete estradiol-17β, also known as estrogen. This hormone is primarily responsible for the madcap behavior of a cat in season. Those behavioral changes begin with the arrival of proestrus, a one- or two-day, minor squall before the storm. Females in proestrus act as though they sense a change in the weather. They become restless and vocal. They flirt with presumed suitors of either sex, not to mention the occasional human. They tread sporadically with their hind feet. They often become remarkably affectionate toward table

An attractive, young Birman striking a well-framed pose.

legs and sofa corners. Some females may allow males to mount them during proestrus, but penetration is generally reserved for after the prom.

In a day or two, proestrus gives way to full-tilt estrus, and the female is ready for serious courtship. She advertises her tractability by howling frequently day and night and by slinking about in the lordosis posture: Front to the ground, rear in the air, tail swept recklessly to the side. She is also apt to scurry out of doors if she is not properly chaperoned at this stage. If she manages to escape—and if she and her owner are fortunate—she will return looking like something the cat dragged in and incubating a litter of kittens. If her owner is not so fortunate, the cat will not return at all. (The estrogen that inspires a female's seasonal display also acts on the higher centers of the brain to prompt ovulation, the release of eggs by the ovaries.)

But observe the word *prompt*. A quart of estrogen would be insufficient, by itself, to initiate this process. Unlike all other mammals but the rabbit, ferret, and mink, the cat is an induced or reflex ovulator—no copulation, no ovulation. Therefore, the estrogen released by the ovaries as their follicles mature cannot do its ultimate job unless the male cat, ultimately, has done his. Only if the male achieves adequate penetration do the nerve endings in the cervix direct a message to the brain. This message, passed on by the brain, instructs the mature follicles to rupture and yield up their eggs. This normally occurs 25 to 36 hours after mating, but it can occur as many as 50 hours later. Once the eggs have been set free, they travel down the fallopian tubes, wherein they rendezvous with the wildly swimming sperm, .0025 of an inch long (.06 mm).

Managing the Breeding Process

Healthy, well-adjusted females that have been in season at least once, are beyond ten months of age, and whose forebears have a history of trouble-free deliveries are the only ones that should be considered for breeding. What is more, only those females whose pedigrees—and, in most cases, whose show records—suggest that they have a contribution to make to their breeds should be seriously considered.

Unlike dogs, female cats display little if any vulvar swelling or vaginal discharge during estrus. Cat breeders must observe behavioral clues that announce the time to breed their females. Ordinarily these clues are published in large print, and there is no mistaking their import, but some females write in a cramped, illegible hand. In fact, some females write in invisible ink, more commonly known as a silent season. They do not call,

tread, or otherwise suggest their availability. There is one straight-ahead solution to solving the riddle of the silent heat: Allow the reticent bride to live with her betrothed until their marriage is consummated. This solution, however, is available only to those breeders who own their own males. The novice, who is best advised not to buy a male at first, must solve the riddle in other fashions, usually by finding a reputable, patient, and experienced breeder who will take a shy female in for stud service knowing that she may be staying more than a few days.

Selecting the right stud requires thought and investigation. Ample leads can be found by visiting shows to study the cats being produced by today's studs and the people who own them, by reviewing yearbooks published by the cat federations, and by scrutinizing advertisements in various cat magazines and breed-association newsletters.

In all this deliberation, the novice breeder should be guided by three principles:
- The stud cat should live in an antiseptically clean cattery.
- He should come from a family or a line of cats that has crossed well with the female's line in the past.
- He should be scrupulously efficient in producing those qualities the female lacks. If a female is light-boned, for example, there is little chance of producing heavier bone in her kittens if the male to whom she is bred has produced only fine- to medium-boned kittens as a rule.

Is Your Cat Pregnant?

About three weeks after a female has conceived, her nipples turn rosy pink and begin to swell. By that time, the kitten embryos she is carrying are barely half an inch (13 mm) long. Sensitive and skillful hands—i.e., a veterinarian's—palpating a female

The pregnant Birman female is awash with maternal hormones. Her owner is awash with anticipation.

78

cat's abdomen can detect embryos and the membranes associated with them between 17 and 25 days after conception. Toward the end of the sixth week of pregnancy, abdominal radiographs can reveal the mineralized, opaque fetal skeleton. Radiographs help veterinarians to estimate the number of kittens a female is carrying and, because different bones become visible on radiographs at different stages of pregnancy, radiographs can also help to determine a litter's approximate age and delivery date for breeders who are not certain when their females were bred.

Care During Pregnancy

Not content with a supporting role in the production of kittens, some owners begin adding vitamins, minerals, and all sorts of potions to their females' (queens') meals—or they begin serving family-sized meals to their mothers-to-be. Additional food, in gradual increments, is not required until the beginning of the fifth week of pregnancy. If your 7-pound (3.2-kg) Birman queen was eating 7 ounces (198 g) of canned food each day, she ought to be eating 9.8 ounces (278 g) a day by the end of her pregnancy, having reached that quota gradually. Since the queen's abdomen becomes more crowded as her kittens grow larger, her food should be distributed over three meals a day soon after you begin increasing her rations. If you notice that the dry-food bowl needs topping up more often than usual, measure the amount you set out there to prevent her from consuming more than the recommended 0.45 ounces (13 g) per pound (or per 0.45 kg) each day. Weight control during pregnancy is important because queens that gain too much weight often have fatter kittens, poor muscle tone, fatty deposits that narrow the birth canal through which the fat kittens must pass, and difficult

deliveries. (Just as overfeeding during pregnancy is counterproductive, so are doses of additional vitamins and minerals.)

Finally, queens should not be exposed to teratogens during pregnancy. A teratogen is any substance that disrupts normal embryonic development. Griseofulvin, an antidote for ringworm and fungus, is a teratogen in pregnant cats. So are live-virus vaccines, excess doses of vitamin A, and some steroids. These and other teratogenic substances are always potentially harmful to the developing embryo.

Getting Ready for Delivery

Gestation, the period between conception and birth, lasts, on average, 63 to 69 days after a female's initial successful mating. Sixty-five or 66 days is the usual duration, but viable kittens have been born between 59 and 71 days. Around the start of her last week

A few weeks before she is due to have kittens, the mother-to-be will begin to look for a suitable nesting place.

of pregnancy, the queen begins investigating open closets, drawers, and the undersides of beds in search of a nesting place. From then on, she should never be left alone for more than a few minutes at a time.

Given the choice, most queens would spend the last several nights of pregnancy on their owners' beds. If anyone objects to this arrangement, the queen should be installed in a double cage in her owner's bedroom. The bedroom door should be kept closed, and children and other pets should be kept at bay. With the queen close at hand, even the most comatose sleepers will be responsive to any unusual noises, ratting about in the cage, or signs of distress in the night.

Double cages can be purchased from companies that advertise in cat magazines, and, sometimes, from cat clubs that have surplus cages. Most double cages are roughly 22 inches (56 cm) deep and tall and 44 inches (112 cm) wide.

Provision the queen's cage with food, water, a litter pan, and a nesting box. The top or bottom half of a cat carrier or a modified cardboard box make a decent nest. If you use a cardboard box, leave three sides intact and cut the front side down so that only a 4-inch-high strip (10.2 cm) is left at the bottom to prevent newborn kittens from crawling out. Spray the nesting box with a mild, nonammonia-based disinfectant and wipe it dry before placing it in the cage. Some breeders use cloth towels to line the nesting box; others use newspaper or paper towels.

Many breeders begin taking their females' temperature morning and night with a rectal thermometer on the fifty-eighth day after the first mating. A cat's temperature is normally 101.5°F (38°C) or thereabout. If the temperature drops to 98°F (36.7°C) or 99°F (37.2°C), the kittens will most likely arrive within 12 hours. If the temperature rises two or three degrees above normal, call the veterinarian at once.

About the same time they begin to monitor a queen's temperature, many Birman owners clip the hair around her anogenital area for sanitary reasons, and around her nipples to make them more accessible to her kittens. Claws should be clipped (see page 35) at this point, too.

The Kitten-Delivery List

The following items should be assembled and close at hand before a queen begins to deliver kittens:
• veterinarian's emergency number
• quantity of clean, soft cloths
• supply of clean towels
• small hemostat (presterilized in boiling water)
• scissors (presterilized in boiling water)
• white iodine
• aspirator
• heating pad
• small box
• oxytocin
• Dopram-V
• several syringes
• eyedropper
• clean, towel-lined carrier
• dextrose solution (refrigerated)
• can of commercial mother's milk replacer
• coffee

Your Role in Delivering Kittens

It is difficult to assist a cat in her delivery if you cannot recognize the signs of impending birth. Temperature, as we have seen, is one sign. Others include rapid breathing, deep purring, kneading with the paws, pacing or turning around in circles, frequent, somewhat anxious attention to the genital area, and passing the placental plug. The plug, a gelatinous stopper that forms at the cervix early during gestation to protect the uterus from external

Nothing decorates a sofa like a kitten—unless it's two kittens.

sources of infection, is expelled when the cervix begins to relax in anticipation of delivery. The clear, stringy mucous that accompanies the passing of the plug may appear a few hours or a day or two before delivery.

As long as the queen emits a clear, odorless substance, her owner need not worry. Dark, green-tinted, odoriferous fluid is cause for concern, however, because it may mean that the placenta has broken away from the wall of the uterus and the kitten is in danger of dying from lack of oxygen—if it has not died already.

Labor begins when a queen starts having involuntary uterine contractions. These are usually preceded by rapid breathing, deep purring, and kneading with the paws. Not long after involuntary contractions have begun, a queen begins to supplement them by contracting her abdominal muscles in an effort to deliver her first kitten. When abdominal contractions begin, the breeder should note the time carefully. If the first kitten does not appear within an hour, call the veterinarian, and have a clean, towel-lined carrier ready.

As delivery begins, a dark, grayish-colored bubble emerges from the vagina. Once that bubble of new life appears, the alarm should be reset to 30 minutes. If the queen cannot give birth to the kitten—either on her own or with help from her owner—during that time, call the veterinarian.

Kittens may present anteriorly, that is, come out head first, or posteriorly, tail first. In anterior presentations, if the queen does not deliver a kitten within five minutes after its head has emerged from her vaginal opening, remove the amniotic sack (or placental membrane) from around the kitten's face in order to prevent suffocation. The membrane should break and peel away easily if you rub the top of the kitten's skull gently with a clean finger or small piece of clean cloth. If the membrane breaks, peel it away from the kitten's face. If the membrane does not break, pinch it between your thumb and forefinger at the base of the kitten's skull and pull the membrane away from the skull carefully. You may have to push the lips of the vulva back from the kitten's head in order to grasp the membrane at the base of the skull.

If another five minutes go by and the queen has not delivered the kitten on her own, you may be able to pull it free. You may also injure the kitten in the process. Injury is best avoided if you try to ease the kitten out rather than wrench it out.

After washing your hands, grasp the kitten between the thumb and forefinger of one hand as far behind the kitten's head as possible. If enough of the kitten is protruding, hook it between your index and middle fingers just behind its front legs. At the same time, support the queen's abdomen in the other hand and push upward. Then pull the kitten gently downward. If the kitten still has not been delivered within 30 minutes, call the veterinarian.

In posterior presentations time is more precious because you cannot remove the membrane from the kitten's face. Thus, if the umbilical cord is pinched inside the birth canal, cutting off the maternal blood supply to the kitten, the kitten will suffocate. If a kitten presents posteriorly and is not delivered within five minutes, begin trying to pull it out. If you are not successful after 10 to 15 minutes, call your veterinarian.

Some breeders try to prompt delivery by giving their females a shot of oxytocin, a pituitary hormone that helps to stimulate uterine contractions.

Mothers begin to clean their kittens as soon as they have been born.

Do not attempt this at home without discussing the possibility with your veterinarian, and learning how to give a shot in advance. Oxytocin should never be administered before a kitten is visible in the vaginal opening. A queen can die of a ruptured uterus if she is given oxytocin before her cervix is fully dilated, and it is not easy for a nonprofessional to determine when dilation has occurred.

Once a kitten has been born, the queen should begin licking it vigorously to clean it and to remove the placental membrane. If she does not remove the membrane from the kitten's face at once, do it for her.

Newborn Kittens

Healthy kittens usually move about in search of a nipple and may begin nursing within 15 minutes after birth. In the meantime, the queen will normally begin chewing on the umbilical cord in an attempt to sever it once she has passed the placenta, which usually occurs within 5 to 15 minutes after she has delivered the kitten. Once the placenta has been expelled, the next kitten, if there is one, should appear within 10 to 90 minutes, but the interval between births is not as important as the queen's behavior. If she strains to deliver a kitten without success for an hour, or if a kitten appears in the vaginal opening and is not fully delivered within 30 minutes (or 10 to 15 minutes in the case of posterior presentations), call the veterinarian.

If a newborn kitten is breathing with difficulty or does not appear to be breathing at all, and the queen has not expelled the placenta, fasten a hemostat on the umbilical cord about 6 inches (15 cm) from the kitten. Grasp the cord on the side of the hemostat closer to the mother and tug gently. If the mother does not expel the placenta at once, do not waste time with it. Cut the cord with sterile scissors on the mother's side of the hemostat, remove the hemostat, dip the severed end of the cord into a bottle of white iodine, and try to revive the kitten.

Place the kitten in a clean towel and then, holding the kitten in the towel between your hands, rub the kitten briskly to stimulate it and help it to begin breathing. Hold the kitten in the palm of one hand, face up. Make sure that the kitten's head is secure and immobile between your thumb and forefinger. Place your other palm over the kitten's abdomen with your forefinger over the kitten's heart.

Holding the kitten securely in both hands at about eye level, swing your hands down abruptly a distance of 3 or 4 feet (91–122 cm), pressing the rib cage over the kitten's heart with your forefinger as you do. Repeat two or three times. If the kitten does not begin breathing, hold its mouth open and blow gently into its mouth to resuscitate it. Swing the kitten downward two or three times more, blow into its mouth, swing, blow into its mouth, and swing again until the kitten begins breathing or until it is obvious that the kitten is beyond reviving. Do not think about throwing in the towel until at least 30 minutes have passed.

Some breeders, if they cannot revive a kitten after five or ten minutes, dip it up to its neck into a bowl of very cool water and then into a bowl of very warm water in hope that the shock will kick start its heart. Breeders who have discussed the matter with a veterinarian beforehand sometimes put a drop of the stimulant Dopram-V under the kitten's tongue to activate breathing at this point.

If a weak kitten begins breathing on its own, place it in a small box that has a heating pad on the bottom and a towel over the pad. The temperature in the box should be 85°F (29.4°C). To maintain that temperature, you may have to put another towel loosely over

the kitten, close the flaps of the box, and place a towel over the closed flaps. Give the kitten back to its mother when she has finished delivering her litter, but continue to monitor that kitten for the next two hours.

Some mothers chew each umbilical cord and eat every placenta compulsively, but after your queen has consumed two placentas, you should dispose of the rest if there are any. Otherwise, she may develop an upset stomach. If the queen shows little interest in umbilical cords or placentas, cut the cords five minutes or so after the kittens have been born, sterilize the severed ends of the cords, and dispose of the afterbirths. Be sure all placentas are present and accounted for. A retained placenta can cause serious infection, may have to be removed surgically, and could mean that the breeder instead of the queen will be raising the litter.

After the last kitten has been delivered, the queen will settle in to nursing and fussing over her brood. As she does, inspect each kitten for signs of abnormalities such as cleft palates and umbilical hernias.

At this point, some breeders give their queens a shot of oxytocin to expel any placental material that might have been retained during delivery. Check with your veterinarian in advance about the advisability of doing this.

Monitor the kittens and their mother for two hours after the last kitten has been born to make sure all kittens are nursing normally and the temperature in the kitten box is high enough to prevent chilling. Kittens should begin nursing no later than two hours after they have been born. If a kitten appears too weak to nurse, you may have to tube feed it (see Supplemental Feeding, page 84).

Maintain the temperature in the kittening box at 85°F (29.4°C) by putting a heating pad under the towel in the box if necessary. Kittens' homeostatic mechanisms, which regulate their body temperature, are not completely functional at birth. Normally an attentive queen's body heat is enough to maintain kittens' temperature at the normal 100 to 101°F (37.8–38.3°C). After two weeks, the temperature in the nesting box can be reduced to 80°F (26.7°C).

Neonatal Kitten Development

A kitten's earliest days are unwaveringly simple. Kittens begin nursing within two hours after they are born, and they nurse almost hourly for the first day or two. In fact, they have only two operating modes at that point in their lives—nursing and sleeping, which they execute in a one-to-three ratio.

Kittens weigh, on average, 3.1 to 3.9 ounces (90 to 100 g) at birth. During their first 24 hours, they may not gain weight. They may, indeed, lose a few grams. After that, however, they should gain half an ounce (15 g) daily until

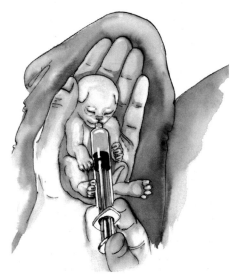

Weak or sickly kittens may have to be fed by hand.

they are one week old, by which time they should weigh about twice as much as they did when they were born. If a kitten fails to gain weight during any 48-hour period during its first two weeks of life, or if a kitten begins to lose weight, call your veterinarian. By the time it is a month old, a kitten should weigh between 14.1 ounces (400 g) and 15.9 ounces (450 g).

To provide food for her kittens, a lactating queen requires 1 ounce (28 g) of dry food or 1.3 ounces (37 g) of semimoist food or 3.3 ounces (94 g) of canned food per pound of body weight each day, depending on the number of kittens she is nursing, their size, and age. These amounts represent increases of 120 percent, 117 percent, and 136 percent respectively over the 0.45 ounce (13 g), 0.6 ounce (17 g), or 1.4 ounces (40 g) of dry, semimoist, or canned food per pound of body weight that the queen was receiving at the end of pregnancy.

Supplemental Feeding

If a kitten cries more than it nurses, or if you suspect that it is not nursing at all, take its temperature with a rectal thermometer lubricated with Vaseline or K-Y Jelly. If the kitten's temperature is below 97°F (36.1°C), take it away from its mother and put it in a small box with a heating pad inside. When a kitten's body temperature falls below 97°F (36.1°C), the enzymes in the kitten's stomach do not function well enough to digest milk. The kitten should be fed two cc's of warmed (98°F [36.7°C]) dextrose solution every few hours, and the kitten's veterinarian should be notified about the kitten's condition.

If the kitten's temperature is above 97°F (36.1°C), feed it two cc's of mother's milk replacer. You can obtain the dextrose solution, the mother's milk replacer, and the syringe with which to administer them from your

Birmans are convinced that nothing accessorizes as smartly as they do.

veterinarian a few days before your queen is due. Keep the dextrose solution, and the milk replacer once it has been opened, in the refrigerator.

Monitor the kitten's temperature before each supplemental feeding. If the temperature is high enough, place the kitten back with its mother to see if it can nurse on its own.

Whether you feed dextrose or milk, the technique for supplementary feeding is the same. Put a towel on your lap, hold the kitten in one hand at a 45-degree angle, slide the end of the syringe gently between the kitten's lips, and push the plunger on the syringe a fraction of an inch to eject some of the contents of the syringe into the kitten's mouth. Go slowly, pushing intermittently on the plunger as the kitten ingests the contents of the syringe. Some kittens suck so vigorously they can move the plunger with little assistance from their feeders. If the kitten is sucking avidly, then turns its head away, it is full.

Kittens whose temperatures are normal can be returned to their mothers

after a supplemental feeding, but they should be monitored carefully to be sure they are nursing adequately within an hour or so. If they are not, continue supplemental feeding every two hours around the clock until they begin nursing on their own.

Kittens too weak to suck dextrose solution or milk from a syringe may have to be tube fed. Ask your veterinarian in advance to show you how to measure the length of tube, attached to a syringe, that needs to be inserted into the kitten's stomach. Since tube feeding, if not done correctly, can cause lesions of the pharynx or stomach, it should be attempted only as a last resort.

If a nonnursing kitten with a depressed temperature has to be placed in an incubator to bring its temperature up to normal, check its temperature every hour. As long as the temperature remains below 97°F (36.1°C), keep feeding the dextrose solution. When the kitten's temperature rises above 97°F (36.1°C), feed it a milk replacer, then give it back to its mother. Watch the kitten every hour or so to see if it is nursing properly. If not, feed it two cc's of dextrose solution or milk replacer every two hours around the clock until it is able to nurse normally.

Raising Orphaned Kittens

Occasionally a queen will refuse to care for her kittens or she will be unable to care for them because she contracted an illness or has not recovered sufficiently from a Cesarean section to assume her maternal duties. When a queen cannot function maternally, the owner will have to hand raise the litter until the queen recovers or the litter is old enough to eat on its own.

Orphaned kittens should be kept in an incubator, which can be nothing more elaborate than a clean cardboard box equipped with a heating pad and a few blankets, at a temperature of 85°F (29.4°C). The kittens' temperatures should be checked every two hours around the clock for the first two or three days, and they should be fed warmed dextrose solution or milk replacer as their temperatures indicate. Feed two to three milliliters of dextrose solution or milk replacer at each feeding for the first week.

If the kittens' temperatures are normal for a few days, you need not continue to take their temperatures before feeding. Intervals between feedings may be stretched to two and half hours during the second week, at which time you should increase their milk ration to three or four milliliters. During the third and fourth weeks feed every three hours and give the kittens all the milk they want. Toward the end of the kittens' third week you should begin to wean them onto solid food. Begin with a porridge of baby cereal and milk replacer for a few days, then gradually add dry cat food soaked in milk to the kittens' porridge. When the kittens are about four and a half or five weeks old, switch to a mixture of soaked dry cat food and canned cat food, and finally, at about six weeks, to canned cat food or dry food alone.

For the first two or three weeks you will have to stimulate kittens to eliminate before you feed them. Dip a section of wadded-up paper towel into a small bowl of warm water and rub each kitten's anogenital area softly. Wash the area with a clean paper towel after the kitten eliminates and then pat the kitten dry.

Kittens do not eliminate spontaneously until they are three weeks old. When they begin, provide them with a litter pan. Place kittens in the pan as soon as they wake up from a nap or right after you have fed them. Do not take their front paws in hand and scratch the litter. Kittens come equipped from the factory with an instinct for scratching in loose material. If you simply place them in the litter box, they will soon get the idea.

Because hand-raised kittens have not received maternal antibodies, take them to your veterinarian when they are three weeks old and have them vaccinated with killed vaccine. Your veterinarian will set up a vaccination schedule for the kittens at that time (see The Importance of Vaccinations, page 50).

If raising kittens by hand sounds like work, it is. During three or four sleep-deprived, trying weeks, your determination and discipline will be all that stands between life and death for the kittens. But you decided to bring them into the world, so you are responsible for seeing them into it.

When you have hand raised a litter successfully, the kittens' progress is a bountiful reward. What is more, the kittens you have nurtured faithfully will be among the best socialized, most people-oriented tykes you will ever see.

At the End of the Day

Everybody loves a kitten. Most people are susceptible to the charms of an adult cat. The true connoisseur of cats, however, knows that the essence of the cat-human bond lies in the bittersweet pleasures of caring for an elderly cat. Your knowledge of one another is rich, constant, and stripped of pretense. The trust, affection, and respect you share run deep, furrowed into your relationship by years of living closely together. You have, in many cases, navigated the rapids of her kittenhood together and have enjoyed the sleekness and agility of her prime. Now it is time to negotiate life's final journey together.

Rates of Change

Because your cat is an individual, its uniqueness will always be part of its makeup and of the aging process as well. Not every cat, for example, becomes cranky and captious with age. A warlike cat whom this writer had acquired during the cat's middle years mellowed considerably as she grew older, a fortunate turn of events for the other cats and the two young puppies with whom she shared a home. Perhaps this oldtimer read the following passage from Camus: "To grow old is to pass from passion to compassion."

Just as cats do not all age in the same fashion, they do not all age at the same rate. A cat's biological age, in distinction to her chronological age, is a function of its genetic background, the quality of its diet, the presence or absence of disease, and the tenor of its environment.

If you are a first-time owner of an elderly or geriatric cat, you would do well to remember that no one knows your cat as thoroughly as you do. You were the one who found that special spot where your cat liked to be scratched when it was a kitten. You were the one who discovered that your cat loved playing in the Styrofoam popcorn in which some mail-order items come packaged. You were the one who was able to comfort your cat when thunderstorms sent it scrambling into the most remote zip codes of your closet. Now is the time to use all the knowledge you have acquired together to make your cat's life and surroundings as comfortable as possible. To do less would be to neglect an old friend.

Researchers estimate that old age in cats begins at roughly their eighth or ninth birthdays. According to the following chart, adapted from *The Book of the Cat*, felines are between 53 and 57 in human years at that point.

Effects of Aging

The passage of time occasions progressive and irreversible changes in your cat. Sadly, most of the physical changes are not for the better. As your cat's metabolism slows down and its vitality begins to dim, its abilities to taste, see, smell, and hear diminish. It is less able to tolerate drugs, less able to regulate its body temperature, and is less immune to disease. It requires fewer calories to fuel its body and to maintain its optimum weight. The thyroid, adrenal, and pituitary glands and the pancreas do not secrete hormones as fluidly as they once did.

	Age in Years							
Cat	1	2	6	10	14	20	25	30
Human	15	25	45	60	72	90	105	120

These changes are generally accompanied by other physical and behavioral diminutions. Your cat's eyes may become cloudy, the muzzle may turn gray, the fur may be less luxuriant, the skin may become slack, the muscles flabby, and the spine and hips more prominent. Your cat may also experience hearing loss, stiffness in the joints, or lameness, and will most likely become less active, more inclined to sleep, less accepting of environmental changes, less tolerant of cold temperatures, and, perhaps, somewhat cranky.

With the onset of old age, a cat becomes more susceptible to disease; therefore, the earlier conditions are diagnosed, the better the chances of recovery. The annual veterinary inspection becomes more important in old age, and you may consider switching to semiannual checkups. Naturally, it is important to keep vaccinations current in order to protect against panleukopenia, respiratory diseases, feline leukemia, and rabies.

Nutrition and the Older Cat

As you and your cat grow old(er) together, you may notice that at least one of you is growing in other ways, too. Older cats often become overweight as a consequence of their

Cats are as quick to camp near computer equipment today as they were to sit on typewriters yesterday.

Nothing takes the weight of the world off your shoulders like a cat.

lessened activity and metabolic rate. The signs of excess weight are not difficult to detect. If your cat's abdomen begins to droop, if you cannot feel its rib cage when you run your hands along your cat's sides, if your cat sways noticeably when it walks, or if it develops bulges on either side of the point where the tail joins the body, chances are your cat is carrying too much weight.

Before attempting to correct these symptoms with a diet, take your cat to the veterinarian first to make sure that the excess weight is not being caused by illness. If it is not and if your cat is too heavy for its sex, age, and activity level, switch to lite cat food. Lite food contains 20 to 33 percent fewer calories than regular food does. If you are feeding both wet and dry foods, try a lite dry food for a month. If your cat returns to its baseline weight, return to regular dry food and continue to monitor its weight. If switching to lite dry does not pare away the padding, continue feeding lite dry and switch to lite canned also.

Like weight gain, progressive weight loss in older cats is cause for concern—perhaps even more so. Weight loss may indicate kidney failure, the presence of a tumor, diabetes mellitus, liver disease, or other conditions. If your cat loses weight for two consecutive months or if it loses more than half a pound (0.23 kg) in any month, schedule an appointment with your veterinarian.

Obtaining proper nutrition for an older cat may be a matter of adjusting to changing political alliances in a multicat household. The cat that formerly ruled the roost may now have passed the mantle—or had it jostled from the shoulders. Patterns dictating who eats

No matter what their age all cats enjoy an occasional scratch and stretch.

first, who gets the choice spots in a sunny window, or who gets first dibs on lap time are often renegotiated as your older cat declines physically. When this occurs, it is important to think out modifications that will ensure the well-being of the senior partner: Feeding it alone in a place where its leisurely dining habits can be accommodated, and seeking it out for attention on a routine basis can help it to make a graceful adjustment to its new emeritus status. Your elderly cat may also appreciate a warm nesting spot near the center of family activity or, if it has been in the habit of going outdoors, a chaperoned trip outside once or twice a day.

Exercise and Grooming

Besides seeing to your older cat's dining and social comforts, you will need to see that it is getting enough exercise. Older cats' participation in play might be limited by their willingness to compete with younger cats in the house or by arthritis and muscle atrophy. You can help your Birman to maintain good muscle tone and suppleness, to increase blood circulation, and to improve gastrointestinal motility (the spontaneous movement of the gut) by exhorting the cat to partake in moderate exercise, the feline equivalent of mall walking done by senior citizens. While you and your cat enjoy a favorite game, be on the lookout for labored breathing or the rapid onset of fatigue, which may be signs of heart disease.

Frequent grooming—three times a week or so—provides an opportunity to examine your cat for unusual lumps, skin lesions, or external parasites. Lumps or lesions should be examined further by a veterinarian. Grooming, which can be defined as the art of removing dead hair from a cat so the cat does not have to remove it, becomes an added kindness to the elderly cat. The more dead hair you remove from your cat, the fewer hairballs it will accumulate in its stomach. Hairballs cause more frequent problems for older cats because their reduced gastrointestinal tract motility aids and abets intestinal impactions. For this reason, bulk-forming agents such as wheat bran or a mild laxative should be given to older cats at the first signs of dry-retching, a reliable sign that your cat is trying to bring up a hairball.

And when you groom your older cat, pay closer attention than previously to its nails. Older cats may not use scratching posts as frequently as young cats do to remove the outer sheaths of their claws. Thus, an older cat's nails should be checked weekly and trimmed whenever necessary.

Digestive and Dental Concerns

The digestive tract is usually the last system to begin deteriorating in the cat. Some researchers believe that rapid cell turnover in the gastrointestinal tract provides some protection against the degenerative effects of aging. Nevertheless, older cats are more inclined to constipation than younger cats are. Milk, which is generally not recommended for cats once they emerge from kittenhood, can be beneficial to older cats because it may help to inspire a softer stool. Laxatives and hairball medications should not be used more than once a week, however, unless your veterinarian tells you to do so, because they can interfere with the absorption of vitamins and minerals.

The time to begin many of the added ministrations that make life more pleasant for older cats is when they are young cats. Dental care is perhaps the best example of this advice. Research indicates that daily teeth cleaning reduces tartar formation by 95 percent in cats while weekly cleaning results in a 76 percent reduction.

Your chances of cleaning your eight-year-old cat's teeth, especially if they have never been cleaned before, are not promising. You may need professional help to get the job done at this point, and, by all means, you should seek it. Accumulated tartar can cause gingivitis and weaken tooth structure, making eating a chore at a time when appetite is on the decline for other reasons. Thus, if your cat is young enough at heart to learn new tricks, you should initiate a home dentistry program now (see Dental Care, page 57).

That celebrated cat lover Cleveland Amory once defined a conservative as someone who does not like anything to happen that has not happened before. The older cats become, the more conservative they get. They are less adaptable to—and happy about—changes in the environment. Consequently, they should be boarded out only as a last resort when the family goes on vacation. And if they must be boarded, they should be surrounded with familiar toys and other objects from home to cushion the impact of being uprooted. Better still, arrange to have your older cat cared for at home by neighbors, friends, relatives, or a pet sitter (see Leaving Your Cat at Home, page 31).

Moving to a new house or bringing a new pet into your present house are additional sources of stress for an older cat. Moving cannot be avoided sometimes, but you can avoid bringing a new cat home. Indeed, once a cat is well settled into middle age, at roughly the age of six, the chances of a new introduction going smoothly and of a lasting friendship developing between old and young lion(ess) are slim and slimmer.

While the tariffs levied by age are considerable, so, too, is a cat's ability to adapt its behavior to cope with any incapacity arising from advancing years. As your cat has always done, it will try to do its share to make the senior years as comfortable for you as you will for it. Its measured steps and treasured attentions will lead you frequently to pleasant reverie: of its life and yours, of eternal concerns such as birth, death, commitment, sadness, and joy. What's more, as you muse away an afternoon together, your cat will nod ascent to all your thoughts and never interrupt to tell you that you are not recalling the details of the story correctly.

Farewell

No matter how well we care for our cats, they do not last forever. Time will eventually assert its claim on them. When that time comes, we may have to decide between prolonging or ending our cats' lives. That is a decision in which selfishness has no place. Regardless of how much you want to sustain your relationship with your Birman, if your veterinarian tells you that your cat is in pain and that the quality of his or her life is below standard, you owe it to your cat to end that suffering. Remember, the privilege of owning a cat hinges on a crucial bargain—we must add as much to a cat's life as the cat adds to ours. Obviously, to prolong a suffering cat's life simply because we cannot face saying good-bye is to turn that bargain into exploitation.

If your veterinarian is willing to come to your house to put your Birman to sleep, take advantage of that service. Your cat's final moments will be spent in familiar surroundings. If you must take your Birman to the veterinarian's office to be put to sleep, do not simply drop the cat off there. I cannot remember where I read the advice, but a British woman writing on this subject sternly ordered her readers to stand by their cats at the end. It is an order worth repeating. Sinh did so for Mun-Ha (see Legends and Legacies, page 6). We should do as much for our cats.

Useful Addresses and Literature

Cat Registries

American Cat Association
8101 Katherine Avenue
Panorama City, CA 91402
818-782-6080

American Cat Fanciers Association
P.O. Box 203
Point Lookout, MO 65726
417-334-5430

Canadian Cat Association
83 Kennedy Road South
Unit 1805
Brampton, Ontario
Canada L6W 3P3
905-459-1481

Cat Fanciers' Association
P.O. Box 1005
Manasquan, NJ 08738-1005
908-528-9797

Cat Fanciers' Federation
9509 Montgomery Road
Cincinnati, OH 45242
513-984-1841

The International Cat Association
P.O. Box 2684
Harlingen, TX 78551
512-428-8046

Feline Health and Welfare Organizations

American Humane Association
P.O. Box 1266
Denver, CO 80201
303-695-0811

American Society for the Prevention of Cruelty to Animals
441 East 92nd Street
New York, NY 10128
212-876-7700

The Delta Society
Century Building, Suite 303
321 Burnett Avenue, South
Renton, WA 98055
206-226-7357

Humane Society of the United States
2100 L Street, NW
Washington, D.C. 20037
202-452-1100

Morris Animal Foundation
45 Inverness Drive, East
Englewood, CO 80112-5480
1-800-243-2345

Cat Magazines

Cats
2750-A South Ridgewood Avenue
South Daytona, FL 32119

Cat Fancy
P.O. Box 6050
Mission Viejo, CA 92690

Further Reading

Behrend, K. and M. Wegler. *The Complete Book of Cat Care: How to Raise a Happy and Healthy Cat.* Hauppauge: Barron's Educational Series, Inc., 1991.

Carlson, Delbert G., D.V.M., and James M. Griffin, M.D. *Cat Owner's Veterinary Handbook*. New York: Howell Book House, 1983.

Daly, Carol Himsel, D.V.M. *Caring for Your Sick Cat*. Hauppauge: Barron's Educational Series, Inc., 1994.

Fogle, Bruce. *The Cat's Mind: Understanding Your Cat's Behavior*. New York: Howell Book House, 1992.

Frye, Fredric. *First Aid for Your Cat*. Hauppauge: Barron's Educational Series, Inc., 1987.

Maggitti, Phil. *Before You Buy That Kitten*. Hauppauge: Barron's Educational Series, Inc., 1995.

Maggitti, Phil. *Guide to a Well-behaved Cat*. Hauppauge: Barron's Educational Series, Inc., 1993.

Mery, Dr. F. *The Life, History and Magic of the Cat*. New York: Grossett & Dunlap, 1968.

Natoli, Eugenia. *Cats of the World*. New York: Crescent Books, 1987.

Necker, Claire. *The Natural History of Cats*. South Brunswick and New York: A.S. Barnes and Company, 1970.

Turner, Dennis C. and Patrick Bateson, eds. *The Domestic Cat: the Biology of its Behavior*. Cambridge, England: Cambridge University Press, 1988.

Wright, Michael and Sally Walters, eds. *The Book of the Cat*. New York: Summit Books, 1980.